100
SACRED
PLACES

This is a Parragon Publishing Book
This edition published in 2011

Copyright © Parragon Books Ltd 2010

Parragon Publishing
Queen Street House
4 Queen Street
Bath BA1 1HE, UK

ISBN: 978-1-4454-4001-9

Printed in Indonesia

Created and produced by: Rolf Toman
Editors: Herbert Genzmer, Rolf Toman
Designer: Sabine Vonderstein
Picture editor: Rolf Toman
Cartographer: Evgen Lutskevych

English-language edition produced by Cambridge Publishing Management Ltd

Translator: Richard Elliott

100
SACRED
PLACES

A Discovery of the World's Most Revered Holy Sites

Herbert Genzmer

Bath • New York • Singapore • Hong Kong • Cologne • Delhi
Melbourne • Amsterdam • Johannesburg • Auckland • Shenzhen

Contents

Introduction

A sacred place or holy site is one that is worthy of religious veneration or reserved for the worship of a deity. The word *holy* is cognate with the word *whole.* In its original sense, holy meant "dedicated to or belonging to a deity."

Holy places are, on the one hand, natural sites perceived and acknowledged by people as holy and, on the other, places built by human hands for a religious purpose. Holy places are usually where specific events in the history of a religion are venerated. Natural sites may be sacred because the gods have revealed themselves there or because they are believed to reside there, for example Mount Olympus in Greece or Mount Fuji in Japan. Sacred places can also be where the relics of saints or founders of religions are kept. They can be the birthplaces of saints or prophets, or the locations where they received their callings, lived and carried out their work, or died. Some holy places are built by a religious community specifically to glorify or please its gods and as a place where the faithful can perform their principal ceremonies and rituals. Places of worship can be churches, temples, and mosques—but also trees, forests, rivers, caves, and mountaintops. It is interesting to note that mountains in particular, which are often regarded as the abode of the gods (perhaps due to their proximity to the heavens), are venerated in almost every religion.

All over the world, sacred sites are sought out by the faithful of a religion, either because their visits—their pilgrimages—are necessary for their personal well-being, their sense of harmony of body and soul, or because such visits are prescribed by their creeds. Many places have lost their true religious functions and have become museums—Cluny and Fontenay in France, or Santa Maria Novella in Florence, for example, representing the Benedictine, Cistercian, and Dominican orders that once played a key role in the Christian world. The curative power of the Church was, in a certain sense, concentrated on such places where monks, who were members of the Christian elite during the Middle Ages, prayed for the salvation of the living and the dead, preached, or performed their charitable works. Believers visited these places because a sense of salvation emanated from them. Monasteries and monastery churches were hubs of faith and conviction. Merely the ruins of a monastery can exert a powerful hold on visitors' imaginations and bring back to life the holy rituals of times gone by.

This book presents one hundred of the most spectacular holy places of every religion, from every religious period, and on every continent. It describes what makes each site sacred and which gods, divine powers, or bringers of salvation are, or were, venerated there.

The United States and Canada are remarkable for the extent to which traditional distinctions have become blurred over the centuries. The religions of North America's indigenous peoples, whose traditional homelands were the vast expanses of a sublime natural paradise, have become reconciled with the faiths of the "Old World." And New Agers now pay due respect to the religious traditions of the Native Americans as they embark on their own spiritual paths.

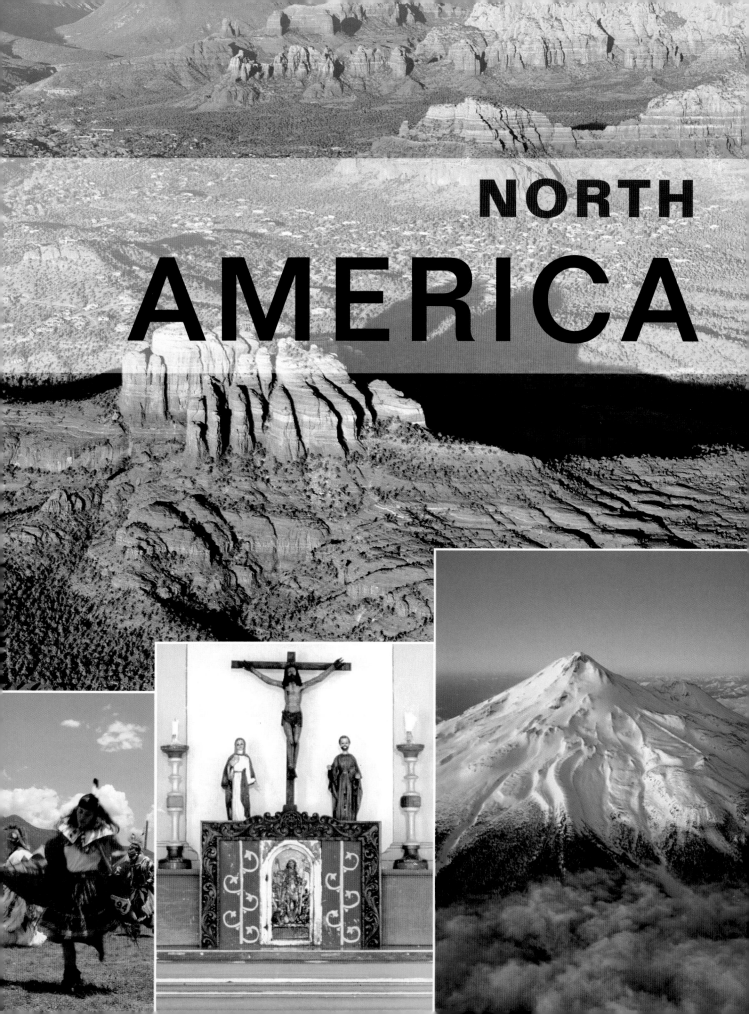

NORTH AMERICA

Crater Lake

CRATER LAKE IS AN EXTREMELY DEEP MOUNTAIN LAKE OF CLEAR BLUE WATER, SET IN THE CASCADE MOUNTAINS IN OREGON. IT IS REVERED AS A HOLY PLACE BY THE NATIVE AMERICAN KLAMATH PEOPLE.

Crater Lake

The lake was formed around 4680 BC when Mount Mazama erupted. This volcanic eruption is thought to have been 42 times more powerful than that of Mount St. Helens in 1980. The entire summit of Mount Mazama was hurled into the air, lowering the mountain from about 9,840 ft/3,000 m to approximately 7,220 ft/2,200 m). The summit then collapsed into the volcano's magma chamber, and a lake was formed in the newly created crater.

The war between the underworld and the above world. For as long as they can recall, the Native American Klamath people have held Crater Lake sacred. The Klamath live in southern Oregon and northern California at a considerable distance from the mountains. Their language belongs to the Penutian language family, which is represented along the entire length of the Pacific coast, and they refer to themselves as *Maklaks*. Members of this tribe used to practice body modification in the form of tattooing and ear piercing. Traditionally, they lived in earthen huts that were sunk into the ground to a depth of over 3 ft/1 m. The natural catastrophe that occurred thousands of years before plays an important part in the popular mythology of the tribe. According to legend, there were once two chieftains—

Left-hand page: This aerial photograph provides a bird's-eye view of Crater Lake, which is famous for its enormous depth and clear blue water.

Right: A number of waterfalls cascade into the lake. Their roar provides the perfect counterpoint to the stillness of the surroundings.

Llao from the underworld and Skell from the above world. A war raged between them until Llao's domain, Mount Mazama, was destroyed. Ever since, Crater Lake has been regarded by the Klamath tribe as a sacred and spiritual place shrouded in mystery.

For the Klamath, it is the home of demons, monsters, and spirits. They only visit its shores to embark on astral journeys in a state of trance and to perform specific rituals. According to the anthropologist Leslie Spier, writing in the 1920s, a man once lost his son and then swam in the lake. Before the day was over, he had become a shaman.

Another ritual performed at Crater Lake is one in which members of the Klamath tribe ascend the walls of the caldera—no mean feat in itself—and then run back down to the lakeside. It is believed that those who do not fall are endowed with special spiritual powers. Rituals of this kind are generally performed in groups, often as initiation rites. To this day the lake represents an attraction for members of the Klamath tribe, who perform their sacred rituals here, but it has also become an important destination for followers of New Age beliefs.

FACT FILE

At nearly 2,000 ft/600 m, Crater Lake is the deepest lake in the United States and the seventh deepest in the world. It is also the world's deepest lake situated above sea level. Two islands were formed during the volcanic eruption: Wizard Island and Phantom Ship Island.

1853
The first white explorers discover Crater Lake.
1954
The Klamath tribe loses federal recognition as a Native American tribe.
1986
The Klamath tribe regains federal recognition as a Native American tribe.

Left: The lake shrouded in mist—the perfect setting for cosmic states of mind such as those sought by New Age devotees.

Above: Once inhabited, Monk's Mound is Cahokia's largest earthen pyramid.

ILLINOIS, UNITED STATES

Cahokia

AROUND AD 1000, TRADE STARTED TO BRING THE PEOPLE OF NORTH AMERICA CLOSER TOGETHER. THE CENTER OF WHAT IS KNOWN AS MISSISSIPPIAN CULTURE WAS CAHOKIA, THE CONTINENT'S ONLY PREHISTORIC CITY.

FACT FILE

The city was inhabited during the Mississippian period between AD 800 and 1400, and consisted of around 120 earthworks. During its golden age, between 1050 and 1150, it was home to around 20,000 people. Monk's Mound is the biggest earthen pyramid in North America.
1982
Inscribed as a UNESCO (United Nations Educational, Scientific, and Cultural Organization) World Heritage Site.
Area: 12 acres/5 ha
Height: 100 ft/30 m

Approximately 3 miles/5 km from the Mississippi River, on the side opposite the modern city of St. Louis, lies the site of what was once the largest and only city on the continent of North America: Cahokia. Cahokia was inhabited for 600 years and was the center of Mississippian culture between AD 850 and 1150. The city covered some 5 square miles/13 sq km. It consisted of hundreds of flat-topped pyramids, round burial mounds and houses, and was ringed around with wooden palisades. The city was inhabited by the religious elite, whose needs were supplied by farmers, hunters, builders, and traders living in wigwams and huts in the surrounding area.

The supreme secular and religious leader of this settlement was the "Great Sun," who lived on Monk's Mound, the highest of the pyramid-shaped hills. The Great Sun was the ruler of all the Mississippian peoples, whose rituals included human sacrifice. Cahokia laid the foundations for the religious and cultural practices of many later Native American tribes, long before European settlers discovered and took possession of the continent.

The people of the city of Cahokia descended in a direct line from the Adena tribes of Ohio, who as early as 1000 BC had buried their dead in dome-shaped earthen graves—along with burial gifts of food, tools, and jewelry.

Serpent Mound

SERPENT MOUND, AN EARTH SCULPTURE IN THE FORM OF A LONG TWISTING SNAKE, WAS A SITE SACRED TO NORTH AMERICA'S EARLY INHABITANTS, AND IS NOW VISITED OFTEN BY NEW AGE BELIEVERS.

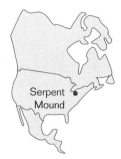

Serpent Mound

Serpent Mound features mounded earth in the shape of a winding snake with wide-open jaws eating an egg. This effigy earthwork has been dated to between the tenth and twelfth centuries, and is thought to have been created by the Fort Ancient people who lived along the Ohio River and its tributaries from around 950 BC. The exact purpose of Serpent Mound remains unknown. However, evidence of burning has been discovered within the egg, which has led to the conclusion that this was the center of a place of ritual in which burnt offerings were presented to the gods. Many archaeologists regard the snake itself, symbolizing the sacred vibrations and forces of the earth, as a gift to the gods and believe that it may have been designed to ward off evil spirits. It is believed that an earth goddess or earth god was worshipped here.

Today, Serpent Mound is a site of pilgrimage and meditation for followers of New Age beliefs, who venerate the twisting snake as an earthly reflection of the constellation Ursa Minor (the Little Dipper) and therefore as a symbol of the flux of energy between heaven and earth.

FACT FILE

Length:
1,348 ft/411 m
Width:
20 ft/6 m
Height:
5 ft/1.5 m
1995
Site dated to AD 1070
(radiocarbon method).

Below: Today, the ancient earth sculpture in the form of a snake is bordered by trees and footpaths.

Mesa Verde

THE FIRST DISCOVERIES AT MESA VERDE IN COLORADO WERE MADE AT THE END
OF THE NINETEENTH CENTURY BY TWO COWBOYS. THESE BUILDINGS INDICATE THE
EXISTENCE OF A FORGOTTEN NATIVE AMERICAN CULTURE WHOSE PEOPLE PRAYED
HERE FOR RAIN, A GOOD HARVEST, AND SUCCESSFUL HUNTING.

In 1888, while looking for lost cattle, two cowboys discovered Cliff Palace, a stone complex built into the canyon wall at Mesa Verde (meaning "green table") at a height of approximately 9,200 ft/2,800 m. Comprising 217 rooms, this is the largest pueblo ever discovered. The empty dwellings looked as if they had only just been abandoned by their inhabitants, with bowls, dishes, and jugs (featuring wonderful black-and-white decorative work) lying around. Upon further investigation of the area, the men came across another cliff dwelling, later named Spruce Tree House, where

Mesa Verde

over one hundred people once lived. Where were the inhabitants? What had driven them away?

Testimony in stone. These testimonies in stone to a sophisticated Pueblo Indian culture triggered a search for further ruins. An unfinished complex with thick walls and the foundations of two semicircular buildings known as *kivas* was duly discovered on a site opposite Cliff Palace. At this holy place, a sun temple, the Native Americans who were still living here worshipped their ancestors, the Anasazi. A nomadic tribe had settled here as early as AD 750 and built ever more complex pueblos into the walls of the canyon. Beginning around 1200, they built magnificent structures such as Balcony

FACT FILE

Circa AD **750**
Beginning of Anasazi, or
Pueblo, culture.
Circa 1150
Construction of dwellings
in caves and beneath
overhanging cliffs.
Circa 1200
Construction of larger
residential complexes under
the cliffsides and in Fewkes
Canyon, with 33 complexes
accommodating up to
800 inhabitants.
1277
Mug House extended to
around 94 rooms and
8 ritual chambers.
1978
Inscribed as a UNESCO
World Heritage Site.

Left-hand page: The cliff dwellings in Mesa Verde National Park are among the most important legacies of ancient Native American culture.

Right: Detailed view of Cliff Palace, which is built into the canyon wall. The circular structures, known as kivas, were sunken temples used for ceremonies.

House, one of the most inaccessible of all pueblos, and Long House, which is only discernable when the sun is not shining on its walls. During the course of the excavations, some 4,000 buildings have been discovered in Mesa Verde National Park.

A mystical site. The Native Americans claim the voices of their ancestors can still be heard at Mesa Verde today, and thousands of people make the pilgrimage every year in the hope of having a mystical experience by the edge of the kivas. In the middle of each kiva, which can only be entered by a ladder from the roof, there is an opening known as a *sipapu*, or doorway, into what some believe to be another world. Here, the inhabitants would once have offered sacrifices to their ancestors and been transported to another dimension in a state of trance.

Below: When Cliff Palace was discovered in 1888, crockery and tools were still lying around as if about to be used.

Mount Shasta

SINCE TIME IMMEMORIAL, MOUNT SHASTA HAS BEEN REVERED BY NATIVES OF THE REGION AS AN IMPORTANT SPIRITUAL SITE. IN MORE RECENT TIMES, THIS PLACE OF MYSTICAL POWER HAS BECOME A CENTER OF PILGRIMAGE FOR NEW AGE DEVOTEES.

Mount Shasta takes its name from the Shasta people who inhabited the region. The extinct volcano, with its double snow-capped peaks, was also regarded as a holy place by members of the Wintu, Karuk, Achumawi, Okwanuchu, and Modoc tribes. Medicine men meditated, collected medicinal herbs, and held initiation rites on its slopes, and the mountain was visited by tribespeople as a place of healing and spiritual orientation. Archaeological finds indicate that the northern side of Mount Shasta was inhabited from no later than 600 BC.

The center of creation. The Native American tribes of the region regarded Mount Shasta as the center of creation. The Great Spirit made the mountain before all else, pressing ice and snow through a hole in the sky before climbing down the slope to earth. He then created trees and called upon the sun to melt the snow in order to create the rivers and lakes. He breathed on the leaves of the trees and created birds, snapped off twigs and threw them into the rivers where they became fish, and scattered twigs in the forest where they became animals. According to Modoc lore, after creating the earth the Great Spirit then made Mount Shasta his abode. One day, his daughter fell from the mountain.

She was raised by grizzly bears and formed a union with one of them, resulting in the creation of humankind. To punish the bear for its offense against his daughter, the Great Spirit condemned it to walk on all fours and scattered its children throughout the world. To this day, Native Americans still perform ancient rituals in honor of the mountain. The Wintu, for example, through the performance of ritual dances, implore its spirit to preserve the holy springs.

Gateway to the fifth dimension. Today, Mount Shasta is visited by New Age devotees as a place of healing and contemplation. It is regarded by over one hundred New Age groups and sects as a sacred source of peace and harmony, and has become a place of pilgrimage for adherents of modern spirituality. Many groups revere the mountain variously as a hub of cosmic forces, the landing site of UFOs, the gateway to the fifth dimension, the source of magic crystals, or as one of the world's seven holy mountains. It is also the subject of ancient legends concerning a race of dwarflike beings that live in its bowels and are thought to be the descendants of the inhabitants of Lemuria, a submerged continent that is said to have existed in the Pacific Ocean around 30,000 years ago, roughly where Hawaii is today. Lemuria is supposed to have been inhabited by perfect beings who lived in harmony with nature.

Left: The second-highest peak in the Cascade Range of northern California, Mount Shasta dominates the landscape for as far as the eye can see.

FACT FILE

Height:
14,180 ft/4,322 m
1786
Most recent eruption of the volcano.
1827
Belated "discovery" by Europeans.
1971
Founding of a Buddhist monastery on the mountain.

Below: Monks from the Buddhist monastery visit the town to beg for alms. "Imported" religious communities also feel at home at purported centers of cosmic energy such as Mount Shasta.

Mission Trail

BETWEEN 1769 AND 1823, FRANCISCAN MONKS BUILT 21 MISSION STATIONS ALONG THE CALIFORNIA COAST IN ORDER TO SPREAD THE CHRISTIAN FAITH. THESE STATIONS ALSO SERVED AS BASES FOR THE EUROPEAN SETTLEMENT OF THE REGION.

Mission Trail

The decision to establish mission stations in California, the part of Mexico that extended north beyond modern-day San Francisco, had been made years before, under the reign of King Philip V (1683–1746) of Spain. The purpose of these missions was to preach Christianity to the 300,000 or so natives of the region, who lived there in some one hundred tribes. After the order was given in 1768 to "occupy and secure San Diego and Monterey for God and the Spanish King," Franciscan monks began work on the first of 21 missions in Alta, California.

As the Franciscans moved north, Dominican brothers took over the 15 missions already established by the Jesuit order further south, in Baja, California, following the recall of the Jesuits to Spain.

Misión San Diego de Alcalá. The first mission to be built was San Diego de Alcalá, established by Friar Junípero Serra in July 1769. However, following disputes with the local Native Americans, the mission had to be relocated a number of times. In November, it was burned down by 800 warriors from mixed tribes. Although the process of Christianization began slowly, by 1797 the mission already controlled approximately 125,000 acres/50,000 ha of farmland and owned 20,000

California's missions in chronological order:

San Diego de Alcalá
1769, San Diego
San Carlos Borromeo de Carmelo
1770, Carmel
San Antonio de Padua
1771, Monterey County
San Gabriel Arcángel
1771, San Gabriel
San Luis Obispo de Tolosa
1772, San Luis Obispo
San Francisco de Asís
1776, San Francisco
San Juan Capistrano
1776, San Juan Capistrano
Santa Clara de Asís
1777, Santa Clara
San Buenaventura
1782, Ventura
Santa Barbara
1786, Santa Barbara
La Purísima Concepción
1787, Lompoc
Santa Cruz
1791, Santa Cruz
Nuestra Señora de la Soledad
1791, Soledad
San José
1797, Fremont
San Juan Bautista
1797, San Juan Bautista
San Miguel Arcángel
1797, San Miguel
San Fernando Rey de España
1797, Los Angeles vicinity
San Luis Rey de Francia
1798, San Luis Rey
Santa Inés
1804, Solvang
San Rafael Arcángel
1817, San Rafael
San Francisco Solano
1823, Sonoma

Left-hand page: Statue of a Franciscan monk near the mission church of San Diego de Alcalá, built by Spanish Franciscans in 1813.

Right: The mission church of San Francisco, known as Mission Dolores, is the oldest building in the city.

sheep, 10,000 head of cattle, and 1,250 horses. In 1834, the mission was secularized and soldiers used its church as a stable. In 1862, it was handed back to the Catholic Church and eventually assumed its current appearance in 1931.

Misión San Francisco de Asís. The house of God also known as Mission Dolores survived two devastating earthquakes and became San Francisco's oldest building, a circumstance to which the city owes its name and existence. Although the mission was dedicated to St. Francis, it soon became known as Mission Dolores after the nearby brook, Arroyo de los Dolores. Construction of the mission, the sixth of the 21, began on June 29, 1776—in other words, just five days before the adoption of the US Declaration of Independence. In 1918, a large new basilica was added with two towers of differing heights, a feature typical of the Spanish colonial style.

Misión San Francisco Solano. The last mission to be built was San Francisco Solano in Sonoma. This is where the chain of Spanish power and Christianity, which extended south as far as Tierra del Fuego, ended. San Francisco Solano is the only one of the 21 missions

to have been built (in 1823) under Mexican rule. This simple church is significant in terms of the history of California because it was here that California's Bear Flag was first flown. It could perhaps be claimed that this was the birthplace of modern California. In 1926, the church was bought by William Randolph Hearst, who restored it and presented it to the state of California in 1944.

Right: The relief-work classical columns contrast with the folk style of much of the altar decoration at San Francisco Solano.

ARIZONA, UNITED STATES

Sedona

VERDE VALLEY IN ARIZONA HAS BEEN REGARDED BY NATIVE AMERICANS AS A PLACE
OF GREAT SANCTITY FOR THOUSANDS OF YEARS. IN MODERN TIMES, NUMEROUS
DIFFERENT GROUPS HAVE TURNED SEDONA AND ITS CURIOUS RED SANDSTONE
FORMATIONS INTO ONE OF THE WORLD CENTERS OF NEW AGE SPIRITUALITY.

Archaeological finds reveal a human presence in Sedona since around 4000 BC. After being inhabited by various nomadic tribes, the desert floor was cultivated starting around AD 500 by the Hohokam people, who dug irrigation channels to make the inhospitable terrain fertile. Next to settle in the area were the Sinagua, who arrived around AD 1000. Their Spanish name (which means "without water") indicates that they were capable of growing crops in arid conditions. The Sinagua constructed pueblos, and in Palatki, Honanki,

Wupatki, and elsewhere, chambers decorated with astrological symbols have been discovered, leading archaeologists to conclude that their religious rituals were based on observations of the heavens. Many archaeologists believe that the Sinagua people left the region around 1060, following a volcanic eruption that created Sunset Crater.

The most visited New Age site in the United States. The city of Sedona is home to numerous New Age groups who use the reported special energy of the place to heal fellow believers with crystals, Reiki, or electromagnetic field balancing. Some also offer past life regression and soul recovery. Since the 1980s,

FACT FILE

4000 BC
Earliest evidence of
habitation by Native
American tribes.
AD 1583
Discovery and settlement
by Europeans.
1956
Construction of the Chapel
of the Holy Cross.
1980
Discovery of power
vortices.

Left-hand page: The breathtaking landscape of Sedona and its surroundings is an enormous draw for practitioners of New Age spirituality, who come here in search of healing.

Right: Montezuma Castle in Verde Valley, a long-abandoned 20-room cliff dwelling dating from the twelfth century.

Below: A medicine wheel, a symbolically charged stone circle used for meditation and healing purposes, captured against the backdrop of the Red Rock/Secret Mountain Wilderness in the evening light.

Sedona has grown into the most visited New Age site in the United States. Over four million people visit each year in quest of the spiritual energy of this sacred place. Traditional religions are also represented here, notably the Catholic Church with its spectacular Chapel of the Holy Cross that creates the impression of being anchored in the rocks.

Power vortices. For New Age believers, Sedona's special energy derives from its power vortices. A vortex is a mystical concentration of energy at the intersection of invisible magnetic lines charged with cosmic energy. These channels, known as ley lines, are often associated with the landing sites of UFOs or the spirit lines created by the astral journeys of shamans. Ley lines and their points of intersection are mapped by dowsers in order to allow believers to meditate, or undergo spiritual or physical healing there. The four most famous vortices are Bell Rock, Airport Mesa, Cathedral Rock, and Boynton Canyon.

Superstition Mountain

SUPERSTITION MOUNTAIN, LOCATED EAST OF PHOENIX, SOARS ABOVE THE ARIZONAN
WILDERNESS TO A HEIGHT OF APPROXIMATELY 3,300 FT/1,000 M. THIS SACRED AND
ENCHANTED PLACE IS THE SUBJECT OF NUMEROUS MYTHS AND LEGENDS CONCERNING
LOST TREASURE, AND IS A MEETING PLACE OF ANCIENT AND MODERN BELIEFS.

Superstition Mountain in the Arizonan desert is twenty-nine million years old. Archaeological finds indicate that this wild place has been inhabited for some 9,000 years. The original settlers were followed by the Salado, Hohokam, Pima, and Apache Indians, who were in turn succeeded by the Spanish conquerors and Mexican gold hunters.

A jagged monolith. Like all high landmasses, Superstition Mountain is regarded by Native Americans as sacred and has been given many different names. The Pima named it Ka-Katak-

Tami, meaning "crooked-top mountain." The name Superstition Mountain was invented by the farmers of Salt River Valley as a result of the many fearful stories and legends they had been told by the local Native Americans, which they dismissed as mere superstition. Indeed, there is no other area of North America in which such an abundance of myths and legends revolve around a mountain. The Pima believe that evil spirits caused thunder to strike the mountain. Similarly, the Apaches believe Superstition Mountain to be the home of the god of thunder; but most importantly, they regard it as the throne of Cherwit Make, the creator of the earth, where he bides his time before passing judgment on the

Superstition
Mountain

world. For this reason, an Apache would never cross the mountain. Many others regard it as the birthplace of the Aztecs, whose secret treasure is believed to lie buried within the mountain's depths.

The Apaches also believe that the tunnel that leads to the underworld lies inside the mountain and that the winds that blow from this tunnel cause dangerous sandstorms. In addition to these legends, there is also many a tale of lost hoards of gold and gold-filled mines, in particular the Lost Dutchman's Gold Mine—the "lost Dutchman" in question being Jacob Waltz, who is supposed to have discovered the richest gold mine in the world—and Geronimo's Gold Cave, which is said to contain the gold of the Spanish conquistadors. There have been many reported sightings of UFOs in the vicinity of the mountain, and there is also talk of kidnappings by extraterrestrials, the unexplained discovery of corpses, and reported sightings of dwarflike creatures who, according to some people, live in caves on the mountainside.

Below: Volcanic rock. It will come as no surprise to learn that rock formations like these on Superstition Mountain have fanned people's fantasies and fears in equal measure.

FACT FILE

The total area covered by Superstition Mountain is about 160,000 acres/ 64,750 ha.
1639
Italian missionary Friar Marcos de Niza becomes the first European to visit the site.
1891
German settler Jacob Waltz, said to be the discoverer of the Lost Dutchman's Gold Mine, dies.

NEW MEXICO, UNITED STATES

Taos Pueblo

AROUND AD 1000, DESCENDANTS OF THE ANASAZI INDIANS, WHO ALSO LIVED AT MESA VERDE, SETTLED IN THE RIO GRANDE VALLEY NORTH OF SANTA FE, NEW MEXICO. TAOS PUEBLO IS THE OLDEST SETTLEMENT IN THE UNITED STATES.

The village of Taos was discovered in 1540 by a Spanish expedition in search of gold. In their dispatches, the Spanish reported that Taos was the most densely populated village in the land. Most of its houses were built between the year AD 1000 and the time it was discovered by the Spanish. Since then, this place, with its adobe dwellings, has hardly changed and still makes do without electricity. The Taos Indians farm the land and breed horses and cattle. They are extremely religious and tradition-conscious, and live in close harmony with nature. This harmony must not be disrupted, for in the Taos world view, disharmony jeopardizes the continuance of human life. Only legend has an answer to the question of why the Taos Indians first came here so long ago. It is said that an eagle led them into this fertile valley and laid two eggs, one on either side of the Rio Pueblo, which runs between the two sides of the village. The Eagle Dance remains a sacred ritual in Taos today and is performed at the village's most hallowed site next to Blue Lake, the source of the Rio Pueblo. Like the kivas, in which other rituals take place, Blue Lake is off limits to non-tribespeople.

Christianization as a form of warfare. In 1598, Philip II of Spain decreed that the region should be

FACT FILE

The region was settled by the Anasazi Indians from the eleventh century onward.
1540–42
Francisco Vázquez de Coronado arrives, looking for gold in the name of Spain.
1598
Start of Spanish colonization and conversion to Christianity.
1848
End of the Mexican-American War.
1992
Inscribed as a UNESCO World Heritage Site.

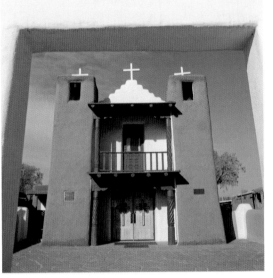

Right: Church of San Geronimo. Forced Christianization during the seventeenth and eighteenth centuries led to the building of a number of churches.

colonized and divided between the conquerors. The Spanish soldiers were accompanied by Franciscan monks, who performed forced baptisms and destroyed all "pagan" symbols. The process of Christianizing the local people developed into a form of warfare that involved forced conversion. In 1680, there was an uprising. All the local tribes revolted against the Spanish and ultimately drove them out—but only for 12 years, after which the Spanish invaded once more. When the US government resettled the Native Americans in reservations in the nineteenth century, Taos Pueblo was spared as it was considered too remote and insufficiently productive, and therefore of no interest during the westward expansion. This allowed the Taos Indians to preserve their ancient lifestyle.

Above: Inhabitants of Taos dancing. The Eagle Dance is still performed here as a sacred ritual.

Right: The appearance of the village, with its adobe dwellings, has changed little over the centuries.

Chimayó

EL SANTUARIO DE CHIMAYÓ WAS BUILT ON SACRED GROUND ENDOWED WITH
MYSTERIOUS HEALING POWERS. THIS LEGENDARY ADOBE CHURCH IS PROBABLY
NEW MEXICO'S MOST VISITED PLACE OF WORSHIP.

At the beginning of the nineteenth century, Don Bernardo Abeyta, a monk and member of the Nuestro Padre Jesús Nazareno brotherhood, left Chimayó to go to the Sangre de Cristo Mountains on Good Friday to perform the customary penitences. All of a sudden, he saw a bright light on a mountainside in the vicinity of the Santa Cruz River. When he arrived at the spot, he realized that the light was coming out of the ground, so he began to dig. He soon discovered a mysterious cross. Leaving the cross where he had found it, he went to Sebastian Alvarez, the village priest. They returned to the place accompanied by a group of villagers and processed back to the village with the cross, which they put on display in a niche in the church. The next day, the cross had disappeared and was found in the hole on the mountainside where it had originally been discovered. The same thing happened a second time. The villagers believed the Lord had spoken, and they raised a chapel over the spot in order to house the cross. This chapel was soon given the name Our Lord of Esquipulas.

Not long afterward, there were reports of miraculous healings taking place at the chapel, and the number of visiting pilgrims became so great that the chapel was

FACT FILE

1680–92
The first settlers from Spain arrive in Chimayó Valley.
1740
Plaza de San Buenaventura (now Plaza del Cerro) is laid out as a fort.
1810
The cross is found by a monk in the desert.
1814–16
The church is constructed.
1929
El Santuario is presented to the Archdiocese of Santa Fe.

Left-hand page and below: El Santuario de Chimayó is one of the finest adobe complexes in New Mexico. In front of the small church is a walled courtyard.

replaced by a larger church, El Santuario de Chimayó, which still stands today.

Holy earth. The cross can still be found in its niche in the altar wall of the church. During Holy Week, over 300,000 pilgrims make their way to Chimayó to pray to God, ask for peace, fulfill a vow, or simply feel the healing powers of this holy place. They visit the sanctuary and take away some of the sacred soil in which the cross was found. Thousands of people have been cured of physical or spiritual suffering here, making it one of the most renowned pilgrimage sites in the United States.

The walls of the sanctuary are decorated with crutches, photographs, and letters of gratitude from the cured. For a long time, the church was privately owned, but it was later purchased by a group of Santa Fe citizens and presented to the Archdiocese of Santa Fe. In 1970, the sanctuary was designated a National Historic Landmark.

Above: The famous cross, which attracts flocks of pilgrims to Chimayó, takes pride of place in the altar wall of the church.

HAWAII, UNITED STATES

Haleakalã

HALEAKALÃ IS THE NAME OF THE CRATER ON THE SUMMIT OF EASTERN
MAUI, ONE OF THE YOUNGER ISLANDS IN THE HAWAIIAN ARCHIPELAGO.
THE CRATER WAS A SACRED SITE TO THE POLYNESIANS, WHO WORSHIPPED
THEIR ANCESTORS THERE.

Haleakalã

FACT FILE

Height above sea level
10,023 ft/3,055 m
Height above the seabed
29,856 ft/9,100 m
Ninety-seven percent of
the Haleakalã range lies
under water.
1790
Date of the last eruption.

The volcano that makes up eastern Maui began to develop on the seabed around two million years ago. It is often described as dormant, but this is incorrect, as it has erupted at least ten times over the last 1,000 years. Its crater is one of the largest in the world: From its edges, footpaths lead down for more than 3,280 ft/1,000 m to the floor of the broad crater.

Haleakalã means "house of the sun." According to Polynesian legend, the demigod Maui captured the sun here and forced it to tarry during its journey across the heavens, thereby giving his mother more time to perform her chores. He did this because the sun had previously been using its spider legs (rays) to travel too quickly.

The discovery of small *heiau* (temples) and altars inside the mighty crater indicate that the Polynesians began revering Haleakalã as a sacred place and the center of their ancestral worship as early as the eighth century AD. Belief in the power of Haleakalã lives on, and even today, it is common to come across leaf-wrapped offerings that have been left on the mountain.

Above: It is not difficult to see why the extensive crater landscape, with its indented cones, invoked a sense of fear in the island's inhabitants.

Pu'uhonua o Hōnaunau

FOR CENTURIES, PU'UHONUA O HŌNAUNAU WAS A SACRED PLACE OF REFUGE FOR HAWAIIANS SEEKING SHELTER FROM THE WRATH OF THE GODS.

Pu'uhonua o
Hōnaunau

Hawaiians who had broken a *kapu*, one of the ancient laws handed down by the gods, could escape death by reaching a safe haven known as a *pu'uhonua*. The offender was then granted absolution by the *kahuna pule* (priest) and was free to go. Not only did these holy places offer protection against the wrath of the gods, but they also provided defeated or injured warriors with a place of refuge from their enemies.

Now a national park, the area is divided into two parts: the Chief's House and the sanctuary, or pu'uhonua. The Chief's House has been restored to the way it looked at the end of the seventeenth century. The two sections are separated by a substantial stone wall erected in the sixteenth century. A reconstruction of Hale o Keawe Heiau can be found here. The original temple was built around 1650 and housed the remains of at least 23 chiefs.

It was believed that the power that emanated from the remains of the chiefs would endow the place of refuge with additional strength.

FACT FILE

Circa 1500
Construction of the great wall.
1818
Chief Kamehameha I becomes the last chief to be buried in the Hale o Keawe temple.
1961
The City of Refuge Park is made a national park.

Below: A palisade fence with wooden totems enclosing a reconstructed traditional-style building at Pu'uhonua o Hōnaunau National Historical Park in Hawaii.

Basilica of Sainte-Anne-de-Beaupré

THE BASILICA OF SAINTE-ANNE-DE-BEAUPRÉ, WHICH ATTRACTS OVER A MILLION
PILGRIMS A YEAR AS A RESULT OF MIRACULOUS CURES ATTRIBUTED TO A
STATUE OF ST. ANNE, IS LOCATED JUST OUTSIDE QUEBEC ON THE BANKS OF
THE ST. LAWRENCE RIVER.

S t. Anne, whose Hebrew name means "blessed," was the mother of the Virgin Mary and thus the grandmother of Jesus. The earliest reference to Anne and her husband, Joachim, occurs in an early Christian manuscript dating from the second century AD. The cult of St. Anne did not take off until the sixth century, and reached its zenith in the late Middle Ages. At the end of the fifteenth century, Pope Sixtus IV adopted St. Anne into the Roman calendar. She is believed to provide protection against storms. At the time of the French settlement of the New World (specifically Canada), St. Anne was widely venerated.

Shrine on the banks of the St. Lawrence. The first chapel was constructed here in 1658 and housed a small statue of the saint that began to attract pilgrims some 30 years later. During the same year (1658), a workman was miraculously cured and a group of sailors who had been caught in a storm on the river were saved when they called out the saint's name. Since the beginning of the eighteenth century, St. Anne has been revered by Native Americans as the "Grandmother in the Faith." Miracles and miraculous healings still occur here to this day, and the small chapel is filled with the

Basilica of Sainte-
Anne-de-Beaupré

Left-hand page: The neo-Gothic church dedicated to St. Anne is one of North America's most important pilgrimage churches.

Right: This view of the interior conveys a good impression of the generous proportions of the church, whose total length is 345 ft/ 105 m and whose transepts measure 200 ft/61 m from end to end.

crutches, sticks, wheelchairs, letters of gratitude, and first-person accounts of the healed.

In 1892, Pope Leo XIII sent a relic of St. Anne to Canada. During its journey, a man was cured of epilepsy in New York when he prayed in front of the packing case containing the relic. This resulted in a significant increase in the number of US pilgrims visiting Quebec.

The neo-Gothic church that stands on the site today was consecrated in 1976 and replaced the basilica of 1876 that was destroyed by fire in 1922. It is split over two levels—on the upper level is the nave, and on the lower level the chapel of the Immaculate Conception.

The miraculous statue of St. Anne. The new church is notable for the beauty of its light, which floods in through 240 stained-glass windows. The ceiling and walls are covered with mosaics depicting scenes from the life of St. Anne, but the focus of the pilgrims' attention remains the miraculous statue of the saint. This statue was carved from a single piece of oak. It is brightly painted and is adorned with a golden crown set with

Below: A view of the crossing, which is richly decorated with mosaics. Many of the columns have figurative capitals.

diamonds, rubies, and pearls. In the arms of St. Anne lies the infant Mary. The church receives its biggest crowd of pilgrims from all over the world on July 26, St. Anne's feast day, and on the Sunday before the Nativity of the Virgin Mary on September 8.

Notre-Dame Basilica

AT THE TIME OF ITS COMPLETION, NOTRE-DAME BASILICA IN THE OLD TOWN OF
MONTREAL IN CANADA WAS THE LARGEST CHURCH IN NORTH AMERICA. TODAY,
IT ATTRACTS VAST NUMBERS OF CATHOLIC WORSHIPPERS.

In 1657, four priests landed at Ville-Marie (present-day Montreal). They had been sent to the New World by Jean-Jacques Olier (1608–57), founder of the Society of St. Sulpice (St. Sulpitius the Pious of Bourges), to preach the Catholic faith. The community they founded was dedicated to the Virgin Mary, and they built their first church of Notre-Dame in 1672. Over the course of 150 years or so, the congregation outgrew its church and a decision was eventually made to build a replacement. The new church, in the neo-Gothic style, was designed by American

Notre-Dame Basilica

architect James O'Donnell (1774–1830). O'Donnell was so moved by his task that he converted to Catholicism shortly before his death. He is the only person ever to have been buried in the crypt of the church. Today, the church can accommodate a congregation of 4,000.

An exuberant color scheme. Not only is Notre-Dame Canada's largest church, but its interior is also one of the most beautiful and richly decorated in the world. The ceiling of the basilica is decorated with golden stars on a dark-blue background, while the rest of the building is multicolored and exuberant. The church contains an impressive richness of detail and numerous sculptures made of precious woods, some of which are painted and

FACT FILE

1657
Four priests land at Ville-Marie and found a parish dedicated to the Virgin Mary.
1672
The first church is constructed.
1824
James O'Donnell designs the new church.
1978
The Chapelle du Sacré-Coeur is damaged in an arson attack.
1982
Pope John Paul II confers the title of "lesser basilica" on the church.

Above right: The large organ has four manuals and owes its richness and variety of tone to no fewer than 7,000 organ pipes.

Left-hand page: Canada's largest church is impressive for its double tiers of balconies, astonishing width, and rich ornamentation.

gilded. The high altar was made by Canadian woodcarver and architect Victor Bourgeau (1809–88). It consists of 32 linden wood panels representing birth, life, and death. Behind it is the Chapel of the Sacred Heart (Chapelle du Sacré-Coeur), which was severely damaged in a fire started by a psychologically disturbed individual in 1978. The chapel was rebuilt and restored to its former glory four years later.

The stained-glass windows are unusual in that they depict not biblical scenes but scenes from the religious history of Montreal. Pope John Paul II conferred the title "lesser basilica"—an honorary title that does not necessarily require a church to be a basilica in an architectural sense—on this church dedicated to the Virgin Mary. The title emphasizes the importance of this place of worship.

Below left: The church facade, which is distinctive for its open arcading below double towers.

Below right: The high altar is set against a magnificent architectural and sculptural backdrop.

The Aztec, Maya, Olmec, and Inca all raised mighty monuments to their gods against the breathtaking natural backdrop of Central and South America. Involving human sacrifice, their mysterious religions, the understanding of which has been lost over time, made expert use of an in-depth knowledge of the astronomical constellations long before such things were known about elsewhere in the world.

CENTRAL & SOUTH
AMERICA

Chichén Itzá

THE YUCATÁN PENINSULA, LOCATED BETWEEN THE GULF OF MEXICO AND THE
CARIBBEAN, WAS THE SITE OF THE RICH AND POWERFUL MAYAN CITY OF CHICHÉN
ITZÁ, THE BIGGEST PRE-COLUMBIAN CEREMONIAL CENTER IN NORTHERN YUCATÁN.

Chichén Itzá

The main preoccupation of the gods of the Maya, and of ancient America as a whole, was to create rational beings who would venerate, nourish, and serve them. This is the creation myth related in *Popol Vuh*, the sacred book of the Maya. Humankind was only created once the gods had devised a special food for it. Quetzalcóatl, the feathered serpent god, brought maize, a symbol of perfected humanity, to earth.

Bloody rituals. By the time the Maya built Chichén Itzá, they were already a highly developed civilization whose history stretched back to the fourth millennium BC. However, they were pugnacious rather than peaceful, and they lacked unity, having disintegrated into numerous distinct tribes. Around AD 1200, the city was conquered by another Mayan tribe and abandoned for good. The priest-kings ruled over their people mercilessly. Their religious rites were bloody and involved human sacrifice. The ball game *pok ta pok*, "team against team," was both a religious and a sporting contest. Chichén Itzá is the site of Mexico's largest ball court. The object of the ball game was to pass a ball through a hoop using neither the hands nor the feet—only the elbows. The captain of the losing team would be decapitated on the court, regarding it as

Circa AD 435–55
Founding of Chichén Itzá.
Circa 1200
Conquest of Chichén Itzá.
1533
Arrival of the conquistadors, who encounter no great resistance.
1841–42
Exploration by the scholar John Stephens.
1923
Systematic uncovering of the ruined city.
1988
Inscribed as a UNESCO World Heritage Site.

Left-hand page: The Pyramid of Kukulcán towered above the other buildings in the complex and was a symbol of power visible from far and wide.

Right: Stone relief of a human skull decorating Tzompantli, where the skulls of defeated enemies and sacrificial victims were displayed.

an honor to be sacrificed to the gods in this way. In order to appease the gods, offerings and human sacrifices were thrown into the "sacred cenotes"—natural sinkholes up to approximately 65 ft/20 m deep providing access to the groundwater, the only source of water on the Yucatán Peninsula (which is devoid of lakes and rivers). Pleas for rain were accompanied by gifts in the form of human hearts cut from living bodies. These hearts were fed to the eagles, while the heads of the countless decapitated sacrificial victims were offered up on Tzompantli (the Temple of the Skulls) in order to placate the gods and ensure the continued existence of the people. All of this was, of course, in vain as the Maya fell into decline prior to the arrival of Columbus.

Below left: A man playing *pok ta pok*. This ball game, which involved the highest possible (i.e. mortal) stakes, was once a bloody ritual performed by the Maya.

Below right: Designed to warn off intruders, stone animal heads guard the Temple of the Warriors, a stone hall that served as the soldiers' living quarters.

Tikal

Tikal

TOWERING ABOVE THE SURROUNDING JUNGLE, THE SACRED PYRAMIDS AND PALACE BUILDINGS OF TIKAL BEAR WITNESS TO A LOST CIVILIZATION AND TESTIFY TO THE SOPHISTICATED CULTURE OF THEIR BUILDERS.

FACT FILE

400 BC
First settlement at Tikal.
Fifth century AD
Apogee of Mayan culture, with around 10,000 people living in Tikal.
Circa 900
Decline of Tikal.
1881/82
Exploration by the Maya expert Alfred Percival Maudslay.
1979
Inscribed as a UNESCO World Heritage Site.

The Mayan people originated in the highlands of Guatemala. Around 1000 BC, they migrated to the Yucatán lowlands and started to build their mighty sacred pyramids some three hundred years later. The Maya were a belligerent people, whose religion called for human sacrifices on particular days and occasions, such as the burial of a ruler. Their leaders cultivated a privileged relationship with the gods, which they demonstrated through bloody rituals. These ritual acts—which involved the torturing and killing of individuals who were often prisoners—served both to placate the gods and to demonstrate the leaders' great power to their own people in order to strengthen their rule. Another

important tool in the consolidation of their power was the invention of writing. By having their acts recorded in writing, the "god-kings" were able to increase their fame and achieve immortality.

Tikal's pyramid temples provided an impressive backdrop for religious ceremonies that were performed in the open in front of the various structures.

Above: General view of the archaeological site, showing a large pyramid and numerous other structures in ruins.

Uxmál

FACT FILE

Location
50 miles/80 km south of
Mérida on the Yucatán
Peninsula in Mexico.
AD 850–925
Late classical period of
Mayan history and apogee
of Uxmál.
1000
Yucatán invaded by
the Toltec.
Circa 1450
Uxmál abandoned.
1996
Inscribed as a UNESCO
World Heritage Site.

UXMÁL, THE NAME OF THE SACRED MAYAN SITE DEDICATED TO THE RAIN GOD CHAC AND LOCATED IN THE YUCATÁN PENINSULA IN MEXICO, MEANS "THRICE BUILT." THIS IS THE LOCATION OF THE PYRAMID OF THE MAGICIAN, THE MOST IMPRESSIVE OF ALL MAYAN PYRAMIDS.

The city of Uxmál developed into a thriving center of Mayan civilization at a relatively late stage—in the ninth and tenth centuries AD. Its ruins still stand as wonderful examples of the Puuc style. Puuc means "hilly country" and refers to the area of the same name on the Yucatán Peninsula, where the Maya built their places of worship. Due to its enormous size, Uxmál is believed to have been a previous capital of Yucatán. Although the name Uxmál means "thrice built," the city, in fact, appears to have undergone five phases of construction. Ceramic finds indicate that this site was inhabited before the birth of Christ. The ruins that survive today date from the late classical period of Mayan history—around AD 850–925. The city's most mysterious building is the Pyramid of the Magician, also known as the Pyramid of the Soothsayer, which is unique among the Mayan pyramids on Yucatán for its rounded-off ground plan and extremely steep elevation. Atop the pyramid stands the temple of rain god Chac, whose good disposition was a matter of great concern to the people of Uxmál due to the scarcity of water in this part of the world.

Uxmál

Below: Extensive view of the Pyramid of the Magician (center) and the long Governor's Palace.

Teotihuacán

THIS PLACE WAS NAMED TEOTIHUACÁN, MEANING "ABODE OF THE GODS," BY THE NÁHUATL-SPEAKING AZTECS. IT IS THE OLDEST CITY IN AMERICA AND THE CENTER OF THE EARLIEST ADVANCED INDIGENOUS CIVILIZATION IN MEXICO. IT WAS DISCOVERED BY THE AZTECS WHEN THEY ARRIVED IN THIS HIGH-LYING VALLEY IN THE FOURTEENTH CENTURY.

Excavations have shown that the golden age of Teotihuacán occurred between AD 100 and 600, and that this city was one of the largest of the time. However, the circumstances surrounding both its founding and downfall are unknown. No one can be certain who built Teotihuacán or why it was eventually abandoned. It is suspected that the survival of its population was threatened by a period of drought, although another hypothesis is that it collapsed for religious reasons. Archaeological finds indicate that Teotihuacán was pillaged around AD 700.

By the time the Aztecs discovered the city in the fourteenth century and began using it as a place of worship, it had long been abandoned and, apart from the pyramids, lay mostly in ruins. As the name implies, the Aztecs regarded Teotihuacán as a sacred place and held countless ceremonies there—many involving human sacrifice—in honor of their 13 main and 200 secondary gods.

A city based on a cosmic model. Taken as a whole, the Teotihuacán complex constitutes a perfect image of the heavens. The engineer Hugh Harleston has examined the dimensions of, and relationships between, the various structures, and has worked out that the

Teotihuacán

Above left: Dancers taking part in an ancient ceremony.

Above right: Detail of the Pyramid of Quetzalcóatl, showing snakes' heads and other sculptural ornamentation.

complex reflects the orbits of Mercury, Venus, Earth, Mars, Jupiter, Saturn, Uranus, and even Neptune and Pluto (which were only discovered in 1846 and 1930, respectively). Teotihuacán is a perfect model of our solar system.

The complex is dominated by the Sun, Moon, and Quetzalcóatl pyramids. Teotihuacán is bisected by a north-south axis known as the "Avenue of the Dead" that runs for nearly 2 miles/3 km. This road is lined with pyramids and enclosed courtyards that were long assumed to be tombs. This was disproved with the discovery that the dead of Teotihuacán were cremated. Swiss author Erich von Däniken believes the road to be a landing strip for extraterrestrials. According to his theory, the configuration of the city and, above all, the construction of the pyramids were inspired by "gods from outer space."

Below: View of the complex, showing the long Avenue of the Dead that has been interpreted (among other ways) as a landing strip for extraterrestrials.

FACT FILE

Area
9 square miles/24 sq km

Pyramid of the Sun
Base: 728 × 738 ft/ 222 × 225 m
Height: 207 ft/63 m
Constructed in AD 1.

Pyramid of the Moon
Base: 492 × 656 ft/ 150 × 200 m
Height: 157 ft/48 m
Constructed circa AD100– 350 in seven phases.

Pyramid of Quetzalcóatl
Originally a temple, later surmounted by a pyramid. It is named after the feathered serpent, Quetzalcóatl, a symbol of the connection between heaven and earth.

Left-hand page: Aerial view of the large Pyramid of the Sun. The relative proportions of the buildings correspond to those of the solar system.

MEXICO

Monte Albán

THE CEREMONIAL SITE OF MONTE ALBÁN IN THE OAXACA VALLEY IN SOUTHWEST MEXICO DATES BACK TO THE SEVENTH CENTURY BC. AS WELL AS BEING A CENTER OF THE SUN CULT, IT DEVELOPED INTO ONE OF CENTRAL AMERICA'S LARGEST TRADING CENTERS.

Monte Albán

Monte Albán (meaning "white mountain") is one of Central America's oldest settlements. Until the beginning of the tenth century AD, it was the capital of the Zapotec people. As a ceremonial center, it was influenced by Olmec culture, which can be seen in the figures and bas-reliefs. The Olmec were a Bronze Age people whose capital city was La Venta. By the time the Spanish arrived in the Oaxaca Valley two thousand years later, Monte Albán was being used exclusively as a burial place. The impressive classical-period tombs,

consisting of multiple chambers containing niches for votive gifts and sometimes decorated with colorful wall paintings of mythological scenes, clearly indicate an extensive cult of the dead.

The miracle of light. The first rulers of Monte Albán were probably shamans—tribal princes who skillfully exploited the cult of the sun in order to consolidate their rule and simultaneously reinforce the economic preeminence of their settlement. On the mountaintop, they were close to the gods who had legitimized their leadership—not just in spiritual matters but in economic affairs, too. The sun served as a symbol of the type of state ruled over by the

FACT FILE

Circa 900–300 BC
Probable date of first
settlement by the Olmec.
AD 300–900
Capital of the Zapotec.
900–1250
Construction of tombs.
1250–1521
Arrival of the Mixtec.
1458
Occupation by the Aztec
under Montezuma I
(reigned 1440–69).
1524
Conquest of the Oaxaca
Valley under Hernán Cortés.
1987
Inscribed as a UNESCO
World Heritage Site.

Left-hand page: The summit
of Monte Albán was leveled
by the Zapotecs prior to
the construction of the
temple complex.

Right: This bas-relief is
number 55 of 150
danzantes, which are now
believed to be effigies
of the dead. They were
originally described as
dancers because of their
bizarre postures.

shaman-priests. Furthermore, all of Monte Albán's
temples and plazas were decorated with images of the sun.
A building of particular sanctity was the Observatory,
thought to be the oldest in Central America. With its
unusual arrow shape and pentagonal ground plan, it was
itself a kind of calendar of the solar year. Due to the
particular orientation of the Observatory, at its highest
point twice a year on May 8 and August 5 the sun
would have illuminated all four interior walls.
Consequently, Monte Albán's biggest rituals were
celebrated around these two dates. The predictability of
this miracle of light brought home to the people the
connection between their priests and the gods. The
climax of the sun festival was the sacred ball game, which,
unlike that of the Maya, did not end with the ritual
killing of the captain of the losing team.

Below: The sacred ball court. Unlike the Maya, the Olmec
did not kill the captains of the defeated teams.

Shrine of Our Lady of Guadalupe

THE BASILICA OF OUR LADY OF GUADALUPE IN MEXICO IS THE WORLD'S LARGEST PLACE OF VENERATION OF THE VIRGIN MARY, ATTRACTING OVER TWENTY MILLION PILGRIMS EVERY YEAR.

Shrine of Our Lady of Guadalupe

Within 20 years of the collapse of the Aztec Empire, over nine million people had been converted to Christianity. One of them, Juan Diego, a 57-year-old man whose surname at that time was still Quauhtlatoatzin, was on his way to Mass one day in 1531 when he heard singing. He looked up to see a cloud ringed with light and emitting rays. A voice addressed Diego in his own language, saying, "It is my desire that a place of worship be built here. Go to the house of the bishop in Tenochtitlán and convey to him my wish." Diego set off

for the residence of Bishop Juan de Zumárraga, but the bishop, who was of Spanish ancestry, hesitated, distrustful of the Indian. After this, the Virgin Mary appeared to Diego a second time, but again Zumárraga hesitated, this time asking Diego to bring him a sign from the Virgin. Disappointed, Diego set off on his journey home. When Mary appeared to him for a third time, she gave him a bouquet of Castilian roses, which Diego took to the bishop. She also left an image of herself imprinted on his *tilma* (poncho of woven cactus fiber). The poncho is still intact today—478 years later—and the image is still visible. The bishop was finally convinced on the basis of this sign, and two years later, the first chapel was

Left-hand page: The foundations of the old basilica gradually sunk, and a new church was built.

Right: The hand of a believer touches the image of Our Lady of Guadalupe, the Virgin Mary.

1474
Birth of Quauhtlatoatzin.
1492
Christopher Columbus discovers the New World.
1514
Construction of the first chapel in the New World.
1519
Hernán Cortés lands in Mexico.
1521
The Aztec Empire collapses.
1525
Quauhtlatoatzin is baptized and adopts the name Juan Diego.
1531
The Virgin Mary appears to Diego.
1548
Diego dies.
1746
The Virgin Mary is adopted as the patron saint of Latin America.
2002
Juan Diego is canonized by Pope John Paul II.

erected on the spot where the Virgin appeared. In 1695, the foundations were laid for a pilgrimage church that was completed in 1709.

The largest Mass in history. As a result of the high level of seismic activity in and around Mexico City, the foundations of the basilica have gradually sunk deep into the ground. Due to the danger of collapse, the church eventually had to be closed, but a new basilica has been constructed next door. The new church is an enormous circular structure with a diameter of approximately 330 ft/100 m, which can accommodate up to 50,000 people.

The list of miracles and healings that have occurred over the centuries is long and has made Guadalupe Christianity's most visited pilgrimage site. On July 31, 2002, Juan Diego was canonized by Pope John Paul II during the largest Mass in human history.

Left: The Virgin Mary plays an important role in the lives of Mexico's indigenous Catholic population, who worship her through dance on December 11 each year.

The Nazca Lines

IN 1927, A SERIES OF ENORMOUS DRAWINGS WAS SIGHTED ON THE GROUND DURING A FLIGHT ACROSS THE PAMPA COLORADA OF WESTERN PERU. CREATED BY THE NAZCA INDIANS, THE DRAWINGS EXTEND FOR MILES AND ARE BELIEVED TO HAVE SERVED RELIGIOUS AND RITUALISTIC PURPOSES.

I t is more than 2,000 years since the Nazca Indians, who flourished in the Pampa Colorada (meaning "red desert") of western Peru between the second century BC and sixth century AD, created enormous geoglyphs, or land drawings, by scraping away the red-black oxidized earth of the Andes to reveal the ochre-colored ground below. Burial sites, places of worship, and ruined settlements have also been found in the vicinity. The vast drawings are believed to have been completed over the course of several generations by countless individuals. It

The Nazca Lines

is astonishing how the works have managed to survive the forces of nature for so long, and many people regard the mysterious markings as an enormous and wonderful puzzle. It seems that the desert, located between the Pacific Ocean and the Andes, is subject to hardly any erosion and was therefore the perfect choice of site for these ritualistic drawings, designed to survive far into the future. The images include a monkey, a condor, a human figure with a round head (referred to as an astronaut), a spider, a hummingbird, hands, and trees. But what do they mean?

A ritual site dedicated to the immortality of the soul. Researchers of the Nazca Lines have repeatedly found it difficult to conceive how the huge drawings could have been made so long ago without the help of modern technology. For this reason, the geoglyphs have been associated since shortly after their discovery with extraterrestrials and superior cultures or species. The best-known theory is that of the Swiss author Erich von Däniken, who claimed the lines were made by primeval astronauts as landing markings. The American Jim Woodman developed a theory that the Nazca Indians made ceremonial balloon flights over the markings, which they considered sacred. However, his attempt to build a balloon out of the materials that would have been available at the time ended in failure and, indeed, a crash landing. Joe Nickell, another American, attempted to demonstrate that the Nazca were more than capable of creating the drawings using the tools available to them. He regarded the works as sacred artifacts made in adoration of, and to please, the gods—as ritualistic adornments of holy places designed to help the deceased attain immortality.

Left-hand page: This geoglyph, identified as a hummingbird, is 305 ft/93 m long.

Above: Human remains some 500 years old at Chauchilla Cemetery near the Nazca Lines in Peru.

FACT FILE

Date of creation
Between the sixth and first centuries BC.
Area over which the drawings appear
Approximately 34 square miles/89 sq km.
There are 1,500 recorded geoglyphs, of which 639 have been described, classified, and investigated by archaeologists.
1994
Inscribed as a UNESCO World Heritage Site.

Far left: These spiral-shaped holes in the ground were wells from which water was drawn to irrigate the dry Nazca plain.

Left: The "Spider" is 164 ft/50 m long. More precisely, it is a member of the genus *Ricinulei*, which is only found in the Amazon rainforest.

Machu Picchu

THE ANCIENT INCA CITY OF MACHU PICCHU IS CONCEALED AMONG THE PEAKS OF
THE ANDES AT A HEIGHT OF APPROXIMATELY 8,000 FT/2,450 M. AT THE HEART
OF THE INCA RELIGION WAS THE SUN, AND THE CITY'S HOLIEST PLACE WAS CALLED
THE "TEMPLE OF THE SUN."

The ruins of the lost city of Machu Picchu, located exactly halfway between the summits of Huayna Picchu ("the young peak") and Machu Picchu ("the old peak"), were discovered in 1911 by the American archaeologist Hiram Bingham during an expedition in search of Vilcabamba, thought to be the last Inca city. Machu Picchu is generally attributed to the Incas, although they themselves claimed to have found at this spot the ruins of a city of unknown origins. The sacred center of the Incas' religion was the

Temple of the Sun, and the notion that this place was built by the gods themselves therefore sat well with their beliefs.

House of chosen women. Nothing is known for certain about the purpose of the complex. Bingham wrongly assumed the city to be the Incas' last place of refuge. As many more female than male skeletons dating from the Inca period have been found here, it is thought that the city may have been an *aclla huasi* ("house of chosen women"). Most importantly, it is regarded as a religious center in which astronomical observations played an important role. Part of Machu Picchu served as a residential settlement, and the remainder served

Machu Picchu

FACT FILE

1200–1532
Golden age of the
Inca Empire.
Fifteenth century
Construction of
Machu Picchu.
1911
Expedition of Hiram
Bingham and others in
search of Vilcabamba,
during the course of which
Machu Picchu is
discovered.
1934 and 1940
Further archaeological
expeditions.
1983
Inscribed as a UNESCO
World Heritage Site.

Left-hand page: The city extends along the ridge between "the young peak" and "the old peak" (Machu Picchu).

Right: These modest houses are part of the "Stonemasons' Quarter," where the city's craftspeople are thought to have lived.

as a religious and ceremonial center. The ceremonial area comprises the Principal Temple, the Temple of the Sun, a sundial known as the Intihuatana, and the Torreón, a sturdy round tower thought to have been an observatory.

Sons of the sun. The Inca people saw themselves as direct descendants of the sun god Inti—hence, their chosen name *Inca* (meaning "sons of the sun"). They regarded their legendary hero and founder of the dynasty, Manco Cápac, as the immediate offspring of the sun god. According to mythology, this first son of the sun and his sister, Mama Ocllo, were sent by their father, Inti, to Sun Island in Lake Titicaca with the task of improving the world. Inti gave them a golden staff with instructions to settle at the spot where the staff sank into the ground. Legend has it that they founded the city of Qusqu (Cuzco), the "navel of the world," around AD 1200.

Below: The terraces are believed to have been used for agricultural purposes.

Cuzco

HIGH IN THE PERUVIAN ANDES, THE UNPREPOSSESSING VILLAGE OF CUZCO
DEVELOPED UNDER INCA KING PACHACÚTEC INTO A MIGHTY CITY THAT PERFORMED
AN IMPORTANT RELIGIOUS AND ADMINISTRATIVE ROLE, AND CONTAINED THE
"TEMPLE OF THE SUN," THE MOST SACRED PLACE IN THE INCA EMPIRE.

Cuzco, the "navel of the world" and former capital of the Inca Empire, is situated at the confluence of the Chunchullmayo, Tullumayo, and Huatanay rivers at an altitude of approximately 11,500 ft/3,500 m. In 1533, Francisco Pizarro (1476–1541), the conqueror of Peru, captured the city with the use of virtually no force. When Pizarro and his conquistadors marched in, Cuzco, which is still a thriving city today, was at the height of its glory. Three years later, nearly all the buildings went up in flames during the 1536 siege of the city by Manco Cápac II, who had been installed as Inca ruler by the Spanish. The Spanish refrained from causing any further damage, instead preserving the basic structures with their sturdy walls and building Baroque churches and palaces over the ruins, above all on the site of the Incas' "pagan" shrines. In 1950, many of Cuzco's buildings collapsed during an earthquake; however, the older Inca foundations withstood the tremors. The earthquake also uncovered many previously unknown walls. At its height, Cuzco was a large city. It is estimated that some 20,000 people inhabited the city itself, with another 50,000 living on the outskirts and as many as 80,000 living in the vicinity of the mountain valley.

Cuzco

FACT FILE

1438–93
Golden age of the Inca capital under Pachacútec Yupanqui and Túpac Yupanqui.

November 15, 1533
Conquest of the city by Francisco Pizarro.

March 23, 1544
The capital of the Spanish viceroyalty is transferred to Lima, and Cuzco declines in importance.

1781
First revolt against Spanish colonial power.

1814
Second revolt against the Spanish foreign rule.

1824
End of Spanish colonial rule in Latin America.

1983
Inscribed as a UNESCO World Heritage Site.

Left-hand page: The Incas called the monoliths out of which they built their sturdy earthquake-proof walls "twelve-sided stones."

Right: During the Feast of Corpus Christi, statues of the Virgin Mary from Cuzco's churches are paraded through the streets.

The most sacred place in the Inca Empire. The upper town (Hanan Cuzco) was divided from the lower town (Hurin Cuzco) by the Huaccapayta ("sacred plaza"), which served as a ceremonial festival ground. The most sacred place in the city and the entire Inca Empire, however, and the site of all the Incas' important ceremonies, was the temple Coricancha, originally named *Inti Kancha*, which means "Temple of the Sun." The Incas were only allowed to enter the temple in a state of sobriety, barefoot, and carrying a burden on their backs as a sign of humility. In addition to the famous golden sun disk—a circular human face ringed with rays and tongues of flame—the temple contained royal mummies wearing golden masks, which were offered ritual gifts of food and drink. On either side of the sun disk stood lion statues whose faces were turned to the sun. The sun disk itself, richly decorated with turquoise and emeralds, was positioned in such a way as to reflect the light of the rising sun. Recognizing the Coricancha as the most sacred place in the Inca Empire, the conquistadors destroyed the temple and built a church and monastery over its ruins.

Below: The Spanish raised their churches over the ruins of the Coricancha temple.

Tiahuanaco

TIAHUANACO WAS THE RELIGIOUS CENTER OF A PRE-INCAN CIVILIZATION ON THE SHORES OF LAKE TITICACA AND THE PLACE OF WORSHIP OF THE GOD OF CREATION, VIRACOCHA. ITS EXTENSIVE RUINS REMAIN A CENTER OF PILGRIMAGE TODAY.

Tiahuanaco

In the fourth century, Tiahuanaco was built on the shores of Lake Titicaca, but as a result of evaporation, the surface area of the lake has shrunk to such an extent that the ruins are now some 12 miles/20 km from the shore. At its height, Tiahuanaco controlled an area extending from the Pacific Ocean, across the Atacama region of Chile, and deep into present-day Argentina. For the Incas, this was the place where the god of creation, Viracocha, rose from the depths of the lake and was venerated. Viracocha was the creator and also the destroyer of the world. According to

myth, he caused a flood that wiped out all living creatures around the lake except for two people. In its heyday, the city had over 20,000 inhabitants and covered an area of 1 square mile/2.6 sq km. In 1200, when the Incas invaded, they found the area deserted, having been abandoned by its previous occupants for unknown reasons. Their culture lived on, however, thanks to the Incas, who believed that Viracocha himself had built the city and ruled the world from it. As a result, Tiahuanaco became an important center of pilgrimage, a status it retained for centuries after the decline of the Inca Empire.

Gateway of the Sun. Tiahuanaco's most impressive structure would have been the Kalasaya Temple with its

Left-hand page: The Gateway of the Sun, which once formed part of Kalasaya Temple.

Right: Sculptures of human heads were set into the walls of this semi-sunken temple.

imposing Gateway of the Sun hewn out of a single block of stone weighing some 13 tons/12 tonnes). The lintel of the gateway is decorated with a frieze depicting a deity assumed to be the god of creation or the sun god, holding two serpent scepters and wearing a sunray-like headdress. Some experts consider the three rows of winged figures and symbols below to be a calendar. On June 21, the date of the winter solstice in the southern hemisphere, the Aymara hold their New Year's celebrations here. Over 5,000 people from all over the world, including many devotees of esoteric beliefs and New Age religions, make the pilgrimage to Tiahuanaco to see the sun rise through the Gateway of the Sun.

Decline. Since the arrival of the Spanish in the sixteenth century in search of El Dorado—a legendary city of which they had heard in the legends of the indigenous people—Tiahuanaco's treasures have been scattered throughout the world. The gold was looted and melted down, and numerous cult objects, including, most importantly, a number of large stone stelae, were destroyed by Catholic zealots because they thought these items were pagan artifacts. Other statues were sold by the Church or incorporated into its own buildings.

FACT FILE

Location
12 miles/20 km south of the shores of Lake Titicaca in Bolivia at a height of over 13,100 ft/4,000 m above sea level.

AD 300–700
Classical period, which saw the creation of large stone structures; finds of gold and bronze.

700–1200
Decline; virtually no construction; finds of simple ceramics.

Eleventh–sixteenth centuries
Used by the Inca as a place of worship.

2000
Inscribed as a UNESCO World Heritage Site.

Left: Tiahuanaco is still a place of pilgrimage for the faithful, who bring offerings with them to this sacred place.

The Moai of Easter Island

ON EASTER SUNDAY IN 1722, A SHIP UNDER THE COMMAND OF JACOB ROGGEVEEN
DROPPED ANCHOR OFF AN UNCHARTED SOUTH SEA ISLAND WHOSE 1,000
MONUMENTAL STONE STATUES IMPRESSED AND CAST FEAR INTO THE CREW.

The Moai of
Easter Island

When the Dutch astronomer, mathematician, and sailor Jacob Roggeveen (1659–1729) arrived at a hitherto unknown island on Easter Sunday, April 5, 1722, he discovered a society that had had no contact with other peoples for over 1,000 years. The inhabitants of the island, who called their home Rapa Nui (the "navel of the world"), were organized into clans. The seamen were immediately impressed by over 1,000 stone colossi, which bore witness to a form of ancestor worship that had begun around AD 400, when large stone platforms known as *ahu*

were constructed on the island to serve as open-air burial sites. Corpses were laid out on the ahus until their bones were picked clean by birds, insects, and the wind, and only the skeleton remained. The bones were then buried inside the ahus, ceremonies were conducted in honor of the deceased, and monolithic stone figures carved out of the rock of Rano Raraku volcano with stone picks and chisels were erected in memory of these ancestors, henceforth regarded as holy. Most of the figures are statues of men with stylized heads and long earlobes, and some once wore stone hats. Many have decorated bodies in imitation of tattoos. Known as *moai*, these mysterious figures keep watch over the land and its people.

FACT FILE

Area
63 square miles/162.5 sq km)
Circa AD 380
Easter Island thought to
have been settled by
Polynesians.
Erection of stone figures
(moai) of volcanic rock up to
33 ft/10 m high and
weighing as much as
165 tons/150 tonnes
1774
Arrival of Captain
James Cook.
1864
Discovery of Rongorongo
script, Oceania's only
written language.
1888
Annexation by Chile.
1955–56
Norwegian expedition led by
Thor Heyerdahl.
1995
Inscribed as a UNESCO
World Heritage Site.

Right: The monumental
stone figures and decorative
elements were made using
nothing but stone picks
and chisels.

The decline of ancestor worship. The transportation of the stone colossi and a trend toward the construction of ever more magnificent houses and ships eventually consumed all the island's trees. Without trees, life was wretched. The earth dried out and became unproductive and cannibalism even reared its head, the victims being the women and children of defeated enemies. The people gave up the ahus, their sacred sites, some of which were destroyed and their statues knocked over as a result of internecine warfare. However, the worst enemy of all was colonial rule by land-hungry masters. In 1862, the Peruvians enslaved all the fit men and women of the island and put them to work in their mines. Those who returned brought with them disease. By the end of the nineteenth century, only a few statues still stood, many more having been destroyed by Christians because they believed the statues to be "the work of heathens." A mere 110 inhabitants remained on Easter Island at that point, and the island was eventually used as pastureland and was turned into a lepers' colony. By this time, the island's traditional ancestor worship had fallen to the same fate as its trees.

Above and right: It has only recently been discovered that the moai were arranged in an astronomical configuration.

Conceição Aparecida

THE TOWN OF APARECIDA WAS FOUNDED IN 1717 WHEN A GROUP OF FISHERMEN
HAULED A STATUE OF THE VIRGIN MARY OUT OF THE PARAIBA RIVER. THE MADONNA
OF APARECIDA WAS ADOPTED AS THE PATRON SAINT OF BRAZIL, AND THE BASILICA
DEDICATED TO HER IS NOW THE COUNTRY'S MOST IMPORTANT PLACE OF PILGRIMAGE.

In October 1717, three fishermen on the Paraiba River in Brazil netted a headless terra-cotta statue of the Madonna measuring just 14 inches/36 cm. Upon casting their nets again, they found her head. After retrieving the statue from their nets and standing it up in their canoe, they began to catch fish in hitherto unknown quantities and the boat threatened to capsize; as a result, they were seized with fear and quickly returned to the harbor. The statue is said to have been made around 1650 by Friar Agostino de Jesús, a monk from São Paulo, and ended up

in the river as a result of unknown circumstances before being fished out in 1717. During the time it spent on the riverbed, the statue lost its paint and was discovered as a shiny dark-brown earthenware figure. A chapel was erected in the middle of the town and consecrated in 1745. In 1843, this chapel was replaced by a larger basilica in order to accommodate the growing number of pilgrims attracted by the miraculous powers that had been attributed to the statue from very early on. In 1888, Isabella (1846–1921), the last crown princess of Brazil, gave the statue a golden crown set with precious stones, and an exquisitely embroidered cloak that left just the Virgin's face and hands (which are clasped over

Conceição
Aparecida

FACT FILE

New basilica
Length: 568 ft/173 m
Width: 551 ft/168 m
Height of the dome:
230 ft/70 m
Height of the church tower:
344 ft/105 m
Capacity: 45,000 people

Left-hand page: The new basilica was designed by the architect and painter Benedito Calixto.

Right: The statue of the Madonna was given a cloak and a crown by Isabella, the last crown princess of Brazil.

her breast) exposed. In 1904, Pope Pius X crowned the Virgin queen of Brazil, and on October 12 1929 (her feast day and now a Brazilian national holiday), Pope Pius XI declared her the country's patron saint. In 1979, the statue was attacked and smashed, but has since been restored.

The largest church in the world dedicated to the Virgin Mary. The old basilica of Aparecida ("Our Lady of the Apparition") was extended and renovated several times, but due to the enormous number of pilgrims visiting what had become Brazil's most important place of pilgrimage, a new church had to be built. The new basilica was designed by the architect and painter Benedito Calixto in 1955. Still under construction, it is the largest church in the world dedicated to the Virgin Mary and the third largest place of worship in the world after St. Peter's in Rome and Yamoussoukro Cathedral (Ivory Coast). It was consecrated by Pope John Paul II in 1980. Today, the basilica attracts eight million pilgrims every year, making it the third most visited Catholic place of pilgrimage in the world.

Below: Today, the new basilica, begun in 1955, can accommodate 45,000 worshippers.

Europe is the "Old World" of the major Western religions, many of whose holiest shrines are found here. It is home to the ancient Greek and Roman constellation of gods, as well as to 2,000 years of Christian culture—not to mention numerous Germanic and Celtic sites whose true meanings are lost in the mists of time and still wait to be deciphered.

EUROPE

Newgrange

OVER 3,000 YEARS AGO, A BURIAL AND TEMPLE COMPLEX WAS BUILT IN WHAT IS NOW IRELAND. NEWGRANGE, WHOSE IRISH NAME, AN LIAMH GREINE, LITERALLY MEANS "CAVERN OF THE SUN," WAS A PLACE OF ASTROLOGICAL RITUAL.

The megalithic tomb at Newgrange was built during the Bronze Age, some 3,200 years ago, which makes it older than the Great Pyramids of Giza or Stonehenge. The kidney-shaped hill covers over 43,000 sq ft/4,000 sq m, has a diameter of approximately 230 ft/70 m, and is encircled by 97 curbstones, most of which are richly decorated with symbols. A tunnel extends 62 ft/19 m into the mound, ending in a cruciform chamber with a corbel vault 23 ft/7 m thick that has remained watertight to this day. It has been estimated that the construction of this passage tomb would have taken 300 workers 20 years to complete.

The Cavern of the Sun. For about a week before and after the winter solstice on December 21, a shaft of sunlight penetrates the temple interior through an opening above the entrance and takes 15 minutes to travel along a corridor 62 ft/19 m long, eventually striking a stone decorated with spirals. This alignment is clearly not accidental and begs an explanation. Spirals are believed to be a symbol of rebirth and of the male sun deity. The ray of the sun god could thus be interpreted as penetrating and impregnating the womb of the earth mother as represented by the Cavern of the Sun. It would appear

Newgrange

FACT FILE

1699
Chance discovery of the
burial site.
1962
Start of systematic
excavations.
1975
Completion of the
reconstruction of
the complex.
1993
Inscribed as a UNESCO
World Heritage Site.

that the entire complex at Newgrange was aligned with the sun, making it a place of solar veneration. However, who built it and who practiced this form of sun worship are questions that remain unanswered to this day.

The winter solstice. At one time, winter would take a harsh toll on people year in and year out, and the arrival of the turning point toward summer would therefore be greeted with joy. The winter solstice, the longest night of the year, had (and has) special significance as it represents hope, a new start, rebirth (of nature), and above all, shorter nights and therefore fewer hours of darkness. In many cultures, the new year begins with darkness and travels its course toward the longest day before returning to the darkness of winter. Furthermore, most of the festivals of the major civilizations begin at sunset on the evening before the actual feast day. This is simply in conformance with the rule of nature, for human life also begins in the darkness of the womb.

Above: The monumental barrow was assumed to be a natural rounded hilltop until 1699, when it was discovered to be a burial mound.

Above right: The present-day entrance with light aperture was designed in 1972 by Michael O'Kelly, who led the reconstruction of the complex.

Right: Illuminated passage leading to a cruciform chamber inside the barrow.

Lough Derg

IRELAND

Lough Derg

LOUGH DERG (MEANING "RED LAKE") IN NORTHWEST IRELAND CONTAINS A SMALL ISLAND WHERE ST. PATRICK IS SUPPOSED TO HAVE FASTED FOR 40 DAYS AND HAD A VISION OF HELL.

FACT FILE

Circa 1180
Reports of miracles at this famous place of pilgrimage.
1600
First reports of women undertaking the pilgrimage.
1704
Undertaking the pilgrimage becomes an offense punishable by public flogging.
1790
The grotto is filled in, and a chapel is raised over it.
1846
Station Island attracts more than 30,000 pilgrims.

St. Patrick composed two texts, the *Confession* and a *Letter to Coroticus*, that reveal him to have been a remarkable figure. He was virtually the only early Christian missionary who sought to convert the heathen beyond the boundaries of the Roman Empire. He is thought to have lived in Ireland during the second half of the fifth century AD. By the seventh century, the future patron saint of Ireland was already widely venerated. During the twelfth century AD, the main center of pilgrimage for devotees of St. Patrick was what came to be known as "St. Patrick's Purgatory" on Station Island in Lough Derg. This place was visited by those seeking forgiveness for their sins. It was said that

a grotto on the small island contained the entrance to the underworld. Descriptions of this place of pilgrimage, renowned for its miraculous apparitions (a glimpse of the hereafter), have been passed down from the Middle Ages. The cave was considered to be a symbol of death and purgatory. For the faithful, surviving purgatory and ascending back to earth represented a form of spiritual rebirth. Today, the descent into hell is symbolized by a night of prayer and fasting in the chapel located on the island.

Above: Station Island in Lough Derg has been a major place of pilgrimage for devotees of St. Patrick since the Middle Ages.

Croagh Patrick

THE PRESENT-DAY CULT OF ST. PATRICK CULMINATES IN THE PILGRIMAGE TO CROAGH PATRICK, A MOUNTAIN IN WESTERN IRELAND NEAR THE TOWN OF WESTPORT. EACH YEAR, APPROXIMATELY A MILLION PEOPLE COME HERE AS PENITENTIAL PILGRIMS.

Croagh Patrick

Cruach Phádraig, as the mountain is called in Irish, was a sacred site even before the Christianization of Ireland. The Celts considered it to be the abode of the fertility god Crom Dubh. On August 1 of each year, the Lughnasa harvest festival was celebrated here, and men and women spent the night on the mountain in order to increase their fertility. During the Christianization of Ireland, St. Patrick is supposed to have climbed the mountain and cast out all the demons from Ireland after fasting here for 40 days and nights. According to Christian tradition, St. Patrick denounced Crom Dubh, who had previously been venerated here, as "black" and "evil," and damned and demonized the other pagan deities in order to celebrate his triumph over them. Soon after St. Patrick's sojourn, the mountain became an important place of pilgrimage. Every year on the last Sunday in July (Reek Sunday), some 30,000 people make the pilgrimage to Croagh Patrick to do penance, many of them barefoot or on their knees. Along the route (which actually originates in the small village of Murrisk), there are three stations with their own prescribed rituals and prayers.

Above: Pilgrims by the statue of St. Patrick, the first station on the trek to the top.

Left: View of Croagh Patrick, showing the open landscape of County Mayo in the background.

FACT FILE

Height:
2,100 ft/640 m and 2,500 ft/764 m above sea level
AD **441**
St. Patrick climbs Croagh Patrick.
1905
Construction of a chapel on the summit.
1928
Statue of St. Patrick is erected.

ENGLAND

Stonehenge

Above: The raising of the megaliths and positioning of the lintels is an awe-inspiring achievement in itself.

BEGUN DURING THE NEOLITHIC AGE AND THOUGHT TO HAVE BEEN IN CONTINUAL RELIGIOUS USE UNTIL THE BRONZE AGE, THE "PLACE OF THE HANGING STONES" REMAINS ONE OF THE WORLD'S GREAT SACRED SITES.

Stonehenge

FACT FILE

Initial phase, circa 3100 BC
Ensemble comprised a circular bank and ditch.
Second phase, circa 2500–2000 BC
Became a conspicuous megalithic structure.
Third phase, circa 1700 BC
Two further rings of holes constructed outside the stone circle.
Since 1918
Acquired by the nation.
1986
Inscribed as a UNESCO World Heritage Site.

Derived from the Old English *stanhen gist*, the name of this place means something like "hanging stones." Stonehenge is one of a number of burial sites surrounded by stone circles. The outer circle consists of a row of supporting stones connected by horizontal capstones or lintels. Inside this circle stand ten stones in a horseshoe arrangement, connected in pairs by lintels. Stonehenge was constructed over a period of 1,500 years and many aspects of its history remain shrouded in mystery.

The stones are aligned with the positions of the solstice and the equinox, which enabled the important turning points of the seasons to be predicted. It is thought that priest-kings employed this knowledge to the benefit of those who worked the land, helping them to sow and harvest successfully.

Celts, Druids, and sages. The theory that Stonehenge was a Druid temple has been refuted on the basis that the monument had already been standing for 2,000 years by the time Druidry was active. However, it seems these legendary Celtic priests made this place of worship their own. Within Celtic society, the Druids occupied the status of a kind of intellectual elite. They combined many roles and duties, acting not just as priests but also as poets, doctors, astronomers, philosophers, and magicians.

Avebury

FACT FILE

2600–2500 BC
Construction of the site.
From the fourteenth century AD
Destruction of the stone circles at the behest of the Church.
1648
Discovery by the scholar John Aubrey.
1920s
Excavations carried out by Alexander Keiller.
1930
Numerous stones re-erected by the National Trust.
1986
Inscribed as a UNESCO World Heritage Site.

Below: The village of Avebury with its large circular bank and what remains of its stone circles.

THE STONE CIRCLES AT AVEBURY IN WILTSHIRE ARE AMONG THE LARGEST AND OLDEST IN THE BRITISH ISLES. AS A CENTER OF SACRED RITUAL, THESE CIRCLES ARE AS IMPORTANT AS STONEHENGE.

Including the perimeter bank, Avebury covers an area of 37 acres/15 ha. The site itself comprises a large outer circle (dating from around 2400 BC) with a circumference of approximately 3,937 ft/1,200 m and a diameter of 1,401 ft/427 m. On the 20-ft/6-m high perimeter bank, there once stood 98 standing stone blocks, of which 27 survive today. Inside the circle are two smaller stone circles.

Sacred fertility temple. Around 1720, the scholar William Stukeley described Avebury as a sacred place of Druids and a shrine to the moon and sun (symbolized by the two circles). The moon stands for the female gender or earth goddess Tara, while the sun stands for the male gender as represented by Taran, the god of heaven. In the context of fertility rituals and the corresponding religious beliefs, the circle is a symbol of the female principle and the standing stones are the symbol of the male principle. To this extent, it would appear that Avebury was a sacred fertility temple.

Avebury

Glastonbury

NOT FAR FROM THE RUINS OF AN OLD ABBEY, GLASTONBURY TOR RISES UP FROM THE SOMERSET PLAIN TO ITS HEIGHT OF 525 FT/160 M LIKE SOME PRIMEVAL CREATURE. GLASTONBURY HAS BEEN DESCRIBED AS ONE OF THE MOST "HEAVENLY AND HOLY PLACES ON EARTH."

Joseph of Arimathea, the secret disciple of Jesus and a member of the High Council of the Jews in Jerusalem, was present at Christ's crucifixion. According to legend, while Jesus was in the throes of death, Joseph collected in a chalice the blood that seeped from the wound made by the Roman centurion's spear. After Christ died, Joseph asked for the body so that he could bury it in his rock tomb. He was refused Christ's corpse, but when the body disappeared after three days from the tomb in which it had been interred, he was the obvious suspect.

Joseph was accused of grave robbery and sentenced to 40 years in prison. It is said that Jesus later took the chalice in which Joseph had collected his blood to him at the jail. Thanks to this chalice, on which a dove laid a piece of bread each day, Joseph survived his incarceration. According to the legend of the Holy Grail, after his release, he left the country and traveled to England, where he buried the legendary grail on Glastonbury Tor before raising a church over the spot.

The grave of King Arthur. Another Glastonbury mystery revolves around whether or not King Arthur is buried here. In 1191, the monks of Glastonbury began to claim—probably in order to have their church rebuilt

Glastonbury

Left-hand page: Ruins of the abbey church dating from the second half of the thirteenth century.

Right: Glastonbury Tor surmounted by the ruins of the medieval church of St. Michael.

Below: Interior of the former abbey church, showing Gothic features.

following its destruction in a fire in 1184 and to lure even more pilgrims to the place—that they had found under the ruins of the seventh-century abbey church a sarcophagus carved from a single tree trunk and inscribed with the following words: "Hic iacet sepultus inclitus rex Arturius in insula Avalonia" ("Here lies the celebrated King Arthur buried on the Isle of Avalon"). In 1278, the remains were transferred to a black marble tomb in front of the high altar of the abbey, where they are said to have remained until the destruction of the monastery in 1539. Since then, there has been no trace of them.

Holy place of pilgrimage. There can be few places in the world that are shrouded in as many myths, legends, and spiritual goings-on as Glastonbury, and none with so many energy lines. As if by magic, it has been attracting people for centuries. The mysticism of this place makes it a sacred destination for Christian, nondenominational, and New Age pilgrims alike.

ENGLAND, LONDON

Westminster Abbey

CORONATION CHURCH; MEDIEVAL PLACE OF PILGRIMAGE; ENGLAND'S MOST
IMPORTANT SHRINE; MAUSOLEUM OF NUMEROUS MONARCHS, OUTSTANDING
STATESMEN, SCIENTISTS, AND ARTISTS; AND A MAJOR ATTRACTION FOR
THOUSANDS OF VISITORS—LONDON'S WESTMINSTER ABBEY IS ALL THESE THINGS.

As far back as the Middle Ages, Westminster Abbey was England's most prominent abbey—and one of its richest, too. Believed to have been founded in the early eighth century by Offa, king of the Anglo-Saxons, Westminster Abbey was given to the Benedictine order during the English reforms of the tenth century and expanded by King Edward the Confessor (1042–66) into one of England's most important monasteries, with a royal palace attached. The church Edward built, and in which he was eventually buried, was designed to outdo the Norman buildings of the same period, such as Jumièges. Two hundred years later, it was replaced by the current church, which represents one of the pinnacles of the English High Gothic movement.

The style of architecture is French—a nave with two aisles, ambulatory around the choir, radiating chapels, vertiginous interior proportions, tracery windows, and so on—but with distinct English overtones. These are expressed, above all, through individual forms such as the ridge rib in the nave and transepts, the pointed shape and profiling of the arches, and the multitier arcading on the internal end walls of the transepts.

The facade of the church with its great Perpendicular window (fifteenth century) was only completed in the

Westminster
Abbey

FACT FILE

The Collegiate Church of St. Peter (Westminster Abbey's formal name) comes under the jurisdiction of the British monarchy.
1065
Consecration of the abbey church.
1066
Coronation of William the Conqueror. The abbey has been the traditional place of coronation of the English monarchs ever since.
1246
Construction of the present church begins.
1503–09
Construction of Henry VII Chapel.
1722–45
Addition of the main towers.
1987
Inscribed as a UNESCO World Heritage Site.

Left-hand page: The richly modeled twin-tower facade of Westminster Abbey was only completed in the eighteenth century.

Right: Interior with view of the choir.

Below: Tomb with reclining figure of Queen Elizabeth I, one of the church's many royal monuments.

eighteenth century. The only surviving parts of the monastery—which, like other English abbeys, was dissolved in 1540 and became a collegiate foundation under the control of the Crown—are the cloisters and, most importantly, the chapter house (renowned for its beauty even then) with its central column and splendid tracery windows.

In addition to numerous tombs of monarchs, the church also houses the shrine of Edward the Confessor (canonized in 1161), which attracted flocks of pilgrims during the Middle Ages. To the medieval mind, the sanctity of a place was strongly influenced by the sanctity of the relics it housed. Saints were seen as intermediaries between heaven and earth. The closer people could get to them, even just to their relics, the more effective their invocation would be. Shrines often contained openings that allowed at least eye contact with the relics.

GERMANY

Externsteine

BIZARRE ROCK FORMATIONS RISE HIGH ABOVE A TEUTOBURG FOREST LANDSCAPE
THAT IS OTHERWISE COMPLETELY DEVOID OF STONE OUTCROPS. EXTERNSTEINE HAS
BEEN A SACRED SITE AND PLACE OF PILGRIMAGE SINCE PREHISTORIC TIMES.

The bizarre rock formations of Externsteine, which rise to a height of approximately 130 ft/ 40 m, are both a spectacle of nature and a mysterious cultural monument. This site has been used as a place of ritual and worship since the Stone Age. In the twelfth century, the bishop of Paderborn consecrated a cave in the western outcrop and turned it into a church. On the rocky summit, there is another chamber—only accessible via a curved bridge—which was used for many years as a chapel. On the left of the entrance is Germany's oldest non-architectural monumental sculpture—a relief of the Descent from the Cross, showing Nicodemus on the right, inclining his head toward the bent Irminsul (a kind of tree trunk or pillar representing Germanic pagan beliefs). In the Gospel according to St. John, Nicodemus is referred to as a member of the Council of the Pharisees who attended Christ's entombment with large quantities of myrrh and aloe with which to anoint the body. Below, we see a depiction of the serpent, a symbol of the telluric power of Externsteine. It is now a sacred site and place of pilgrimage for New Age devotees. Witches, Druids, Celtic sects, and esotericists have all resurfaced here in recent times.

Externsteine

FACT FILE

Only the last 13 stone columns are regarded as forming part of the sacred ensemble.

Location
Kreis Lippe in northeast North Rhine-Westphalia.

Geology
Osning sandstone, dating from the Lower Cretaceous era (circa 120 million years ago).

Length:
Over 1,000 ft/305 m from one end of the ridge to the other.

1926
The rock formations gain protected status as part of the Externsteine conservation area covering some 314 acres/127 ha.

The Irminsul symbol. In 1935, an amateur archaeologist by the name of Wilhelm Teudt claimed to have discovered the sacred Saxon relic known as the Irminsul at Externsteine. The Irminsul is regarded as a symbol of German resistance to Christianization. Charlemagne is supposed to have destroyed the Saxon place of worship at Externsteine—and with it the Irminsul—in AD 722, during the Saxon Wars. Because of this connection, neo-Nazi groups have started gathering here in the hope of reviving ancient German beliefs by celebrating the solstice and invoking German deities, such as Wotan and Freya.

Stone Age finds. Stone projectile heads and tools dating from the Paleolithic Age have been found in the immediate vicinity of the rocks, indicating that this place was already inhabited by around 10,000 BC. However, the question of what it was used for in pre-Christian times remains unanswered. Theories include a place of veneration of Germanic gods and, as postulated by the anthroposophist Rolf Speckner, an oracle temple.

Above and right: The rock formations at Externsteine near Horn-Bad Meinberg are a natural phenomenon that has continually attracted enormous interest. In the first quarter of the twelfth century, the bishop of Paderborn,

Heinrich Werl, planned to build a holy sepulchre here, of which the relief depicting the Descent from the Cross—an extremely rare example of Romanesque sculpture in Germany—would have been a part.

GERMANY

Aachen Cathedral

OVER 12,000 YEARS HAVE PASSED SINCE CHARLEMAGNE MADE AACHEN THE
CENTER OF HIS EMPIRE. IN DOING SO, HE RAISED AN ENDURING MONUMENT TO THE
IDEA THAT EMPIRE AND CHURCH—WORLDLY POWER AND RELIGION—BELONG HAND
IN HAND.

Charlemagne (AD 747–814) recognized the ability of the vanished Roman Empire to integrate different cultures, religions, and peoples and harness them to its own ends. Most importantly, he was aware of the power of religion to unite. It was therefore no accident that he built his Palatine Chapel over the ruins of a Roman bath in the tradition of the Roman emperors. This octagonal chapel was to become the religious center of his Frankish Empire and the heart of the present-day Aachen Cathedral. Charlemagne saw the role of king as being the representative on earth of Christ enthroned in heaven. It was Christ who gave him his authority to rule. The construction of his church, on the other hand, underlined his desire to take up the succession to the Roman Empire. As the unifying force within the realm, Charlemagne's Palatine Chapel soon came to be regarded by the faithful as a holy place. The stream of pilgrims became so heavy that the church had to be enlarged over the course of the centuries.

The Palatine Chapel as a place of coronation. When the Romans arrived at the place that would later be the site of the Palatine Chapel, they found a Celtic temple dedicated to the deity Granus, the god of light, fire, hot springs, and healing.

• Aachen Cathedral

FACT FILE

Second half of the eighth century AD
Construction of the Palatine Chapel under Charlemagne.
813–1531
Coronation of 32 Holy Roman emperors.
1215
Frederick II has Charlemagne's remains transferred to a golden shrine.
1664
Baroque cupola added to the Palatine Chapel.
After 1879
Remodeled in the historicist style.
World War II
War damage.
1966
Comprehensive restoration completed.
1978
Inscribed as a UNESCO World Heritage Site.

Below left and right: Interior view of the Carolingian octagon (gallery), decorated in the late antique style, showing Charlemagne's throne.

Left-hand page: At the center of Aachen Cathedral—in reality, an ensemble of separate structures—is the famous octagon of Charlemagne's Palatine Chapel.

Right: In the fourteenth century, the Carolingian apse was replaced by a large "glass chapel" inspired by the choir of Sainte-Chapelle in Paris, which predated it by a hundred years.

They rebuilt the complex with baths for their border legionaries and named the place Aquisgrani, the "springs of Granus." Hundreds of years later, Charlemagne built his imperial palace here, and over the course of the centuries, a ring of radiating chapels was built around the Palatine Chapel. With its octagonal ground plan, Aachen Cathedral serves as a reminder of the fact that Christ was resurrected on the day after the Sabbath—in other words, the eighth day of creation. In medieval theology, the figure 8 symbolized completion, while an 8 on its side symbolized infinity. Reiterating the key number used in the plan, the cathedral is adorned by eight large and eight small towers.

Within his circle of scholarly friends, Charlemagne was fond of calling himself King David. He saw himself as a successor to the kings of the Old Testament. In 813, he crowned his son, Louis the Pious, during a solemn service in the Palatine Chapel. However, it was over a hundred years later that Otto I, with his own coronation in Aachen, started the long tradition that took its cue from Charlemagne (who had been buried in the Palatine Chapel) and which a further 30 German kings followed.

Cologne Cathedral

IN 1164, THE REMAINS OF THE THREE MAGI WERE BROUGHT FROM MILAN TO COLOGNE, THEN THE BIGGEST CITY IN THE HOLY ROMAN EMPIRE, AND HOUSED IN A NEW AND MAGNIFICENT SHRINE. THIS NECESSITATED A NEW CHURCH THAT WOULD DO JUSTICE TO THE SHRINE AND THE INCREASED PRESTIGE OF THE CATHEDRAL.

The importance of the Cologne relics is evident in the fact that after being crowned, the Holy Roman emperors would make the journey from Aachen to Cologne to pray at the shrine of the Three Magi. Not only is this the largest surviving medieval reliquary, it is also outstanding in terms of its iconography and craftsmanship. The design and architectonic conception was the work of Nikolaus von Verdun, the most important goldsmith of the Middle Ages.

The grandest of ambitions. Ambitions for a new cathedral to replace the old Carolingian structure were entirely in keeping with the size and quality of the shrine. In terms of dimensions and craftsmanship, the new church was intended to surpass anything that had come before. The foundation stone of the five-aisled church with transept, ambulatory choir, and radiating chapels was eventually laid in 1248. The plans provided for two west-front towers that would soar to a great height. The stylistic models for both the overall structure and the detailed forms were thoroughly French. Construction, however, proceeded falteringly. The choir was not consecrated until 1322, the south tower had only reached the second story by 1410, and the west front was not completed until the nineteenth

Cologne
Cathedral

Left-hand page and right: View of Cologne Cathedral from the Rhine River. Because central Cologne is relatively low-rise, the cathedral continues to dominate the city today.

To the dimensions of the cathedral can be added one more: The cathedral's facade has a surface area of some 75,000 sq ft/7,000 sq m—the largest of any church in the world.

century—in a Romantic style impregnated with German nationalism that harked back to the distant Middle Ages.

The Three Magi pilgrimage. The magnificent reliquary and new cathedral encouraged veneration of the Three Magi, and the Cologne pilgrimage flourished from the fourteenth century to 1794. The cathedral houses numerous exquisite furnishings, including the Gero Cross and Stephan Lochner's altar painting of the patron saints of Cologne. Preeminent among these treasures, however, has always been the shrine of the Three Magi.

Below: The depiction of the Adoration of the Magi adorning the front of the intricately decorated shrine. After Archbishop Rainald von Dassel brought the relics of the Three Magi to Cologne in 1164, the cathedral ceased to be merely the seat of the archbishops of Cologne and became one of Europe's most important and impressive pilgrimage churches.

FACT FILE

Dimensions of the shrine of the Three Magi
Height: 60 inches/153 cm
Width: 43 inches/110 cm
Length: 87 inches/220 cm
The reliquary is adorned with 1,000 precious stones and pearls, and inlaid with over 300 antique gems and cameos.

Dimensions of the cathedral
Overall length: 472 ft/144 m
Width of transept: 282 ft/86 m
Height of towers: 515 ft/157 m
Area (interior): 66,370 sq ft/6,166 sq m

Melk Abbey

MELK ABBEY IS A LANDMARK OF THE WACHAU REGION OF LOWER AUSTRIA. THE MONASTERY REMAINS AN IDEOLOGICAL CENTER OF THE BENEDICTINE ORDER TODAY, AND ITS LIBRARY OF MANUSCRIPTS IS ONE OF THE LARGEST AND MOST VALUABLE IN THE WORLD.

Melk had been a strategically important location as far back as the Roman Empire. Originally, a fortress had stood on the rocky outcrop overlooking the Danube River. This rocky bluff later became the seat of the Babenberger dynasty. In the *Nibelungenlied*, Melk is called "Medelike." It is where Kriemhild stops off on her way to visit Attila, the king of the Huns. Because Kriemhild's party is impatient to make progress, however, "the guests were served their cup of welcome and refreshment in golden vessels on the road."

In 1089, Leopold II founded a monastery at Melk with Benedictine monks from Lambach Abbey in upper Austria, which had embraced the Hirsau Reforms. The new monastery soon developed into a cultural center with an important scriptorium. At the beginning of the fifteenth century, Abbot Nikolaus Seyringer introduced the *consuetudines* ("monastic rules") of Subiaco, thereby making Melk Abbey the center of the Melk Reforms, which were particularly successful in Austria and southern Germany.

After the Protestant Reformation, which was a time of decline for all monasteries, Melk experienced a revival, both spiritual and doctrinal, in the seventeenth

Left-hand page: The splendor of the Baroque palaces exerted an unmistakable influence on some of the monastic architecture of the day. Melk Abbey, which overlooks the Danube River, is a prime example.

Right: The interior of the abbey church, in which architecture, sculpture, and painting are united in the service of religion, reveals something of the Baroque taste for the *gesamtkunstwerk* ("synthesis of the arts").

century. Among other ways, this revival expressed itself in the rebuilding of the church and monastic complex under the direction of the architect Jakob Prandtauer and his successor Josef Munggenast, starting in the early eighteenth century. The new and magnificent buildings in the Baroque style reveal that the intention behind the rebuilding of the monastery was first and foremost to proclaim the power of the Church from this prominent site on the banks of the Danube.

With its double towers and numerous windows, the abbey church is clearly the showpiece of the monastery. Its interior is resplendent with marble and frescoes by Johann Michael Rottmayr and Paul Troger, who also painted the ceiling of the library. Housing over 85,000 precious volumes, the library at Melk is a collection of all the important writings that have helped to shape Western thought.

The rules of St. Benedict. "Denying oneself in order to follow Christ; chastising the body; seeking not after pleasure; loving the fast"—are just a few of the precepts contained in the 72 chapters of rules composed by St. Benedict of Nursia for the monastic order he founded in Monte Cassino, Italy, in 529. These monastic rules, the majority of which fall under the heading *ora et labora* ("pray and work"), were adopted by monasteries all over Europe.

FACT FILE

AD **480–542**
St. Benedict of Nursia founds the Benedictine order in Monte Cassino.
996
Earliest historical reference to the name *Ostarrîchi* (Austria).
1089
Leopold II gives Melk castle to the Benedictine order.
1702–36
Construction of the Baroque church and monastic complex.
2000
Wachau region inscribed as a UNESCO World Heritage Site.

Mariacki Church

POPE JOHN PAUL II FELT AT HOME IN CRACOW. HIS VENERATION OF THE VIRGIN MARY HAD ITS ROOTS IN THE CITY'S MARIACKI CHURCH, WHOSE VEIT STOSS ALTAR-PIECE IS ONE OF POLAND'S MOST IMPORTANT ARTWORKS.

Polish Catholicism is well known for its veneration of the Virgin Mary. This phenomenon acquired a high profile throughout the world thanks to John Paul II, who died in 2005. "Marian piety," wrote the Polish pope, who was archbishop of Cracow from 1964 to 1978, "plays an integral part in my inner life and spiritual theology. I should also add that ever since my youth, my personal and inner spiritual connection with the Mother of Christ has been influenced by the great tradition of veneration of the Blessed Virgin whose history and many secondary devotions are rooted in Poland."

Mariacki Church

The visit of Pope John Paul II to Poland in 1979 was a moving event for the whole nation. This was the first time a bishop from a Slavic country had been elected pope, and John Paul II was to have a major impact on the entire Christian world. After the assassination attempt on his life in Rome in 1981, he thanked Our Lady of Fátima for his survival. The attack had happened on the same day of the year as the first of her apparitions in distant Portugal, and it was clear to him that divine providence had been at work.

The Mariacki Church and its high altar. This basilica in Cracow was the church of John Paul II, the most famous Pole of the last 50 years, whose beatification

FACT FILE

1222
Original Romanesque church built; destroyed in 1241.
1355–1408
Construction of the present basilica.
1477–89
Altarpiece of the Virgin Mary by Veit Stoss. Measuring 36 × 43 ft/ 11 × 13 m, this is Europe's largest Gothic altarpiece and one of the most important works of art of the Late Gothic period.

Left-hand page: High altar (1477–89) by Veit Stoss in the Mariacki Church, Cracow. The altar has a height of 23 ft 10 inches/ 7.25 m and a width of 17 ft 6 inches/5.34 m.

Right: A crowd greets Pope John Paul II during his visit to Cracow.

was initiated immediately after his death. This triple-aisled Gothic basilica, with stellar vault and double towers that soar above its west front, was built between 1355 and 1408.

The long chancel is dominated by the city's most famous work of art: the altarpiece by Veit Stoss, which features some 200 painted and gilded linden wood figures. The figures in the central scene, which depicts the death of the Virgin, are larger than life. Above this middle section is a representation of the Assumption, while the wings of the altarpiece portray the lives of Christ and the Virgin. The altar was designed to be viewed from a certain distance, and the figures seem curiously foreshortened when examined up close.

On the facade of the church are various tombstones and memorial tablets, including one in honor of Pope John Paul II.

Below: The Market Square in Cracow with the Mariacki Church (parish church of the Assumption of the Virgin Mary) in its northeast corner.

Jasna Góra Monastery

THE BAROQUE MONASTERY OF JASNA GÓRA IN CZĘSTOCHOWA, WHERE THE ICON OF THE BLACK MADONNA IS VENERATED, IS THE THIRD-LARGEST CATHOLIC PLACE OF PILGRIMAGE IN THE WORLD.

The monastery of Jasna Góra (meaning "bright mountain") in Częstochowa is Poland's national shrine and home of the icon of the Black Madonna, the nation's holiest relic. According to tradition, it was painted by St. Luke the Evangelist on a tabletop made by Jesus. The icon was discovered by St. Helen, mother of the Roman emperor Constantine (circa AD 280–337), who collected relics from the Holy Land. The icon was subsequently taken to Constantinople, where according to legend it remained for 500 years. In 803, it is believed to have been given by the Byzantine emperor to a Greek princess on the occasion of her wedding to a Ruthenian prince. It then remained in the royal palace in Belz, Ukraine, not far from the Polish border, for around 600 years.

The icon was supposedly brought to Poland in 1382 by the Polish army as it fled the Tartars. There is a legend that states that during the looting of the city, the chapel in Belz containing the icon was shrouded in a mysterious cloud, enabling the Poles to remove the icon unobserved. A monastery of the Pauline order was founded in Częstochowa in 1386 in order to house the relic. Before long, King Władysław II Jagiełło (1348–1434) built a cathedral around the chapel.

FACT FILE

1386
Founding of the monastery of Jasna Góra.

1430
The monastery is attacked, and the image of the Virgin Mary is badly damaged.

1650
The ivory-and-silver altar on which the icon stands is donated by Jerzy Ossoliński.

1950
Restoration work completed.

1983
Lech Walesa dedicates his Nobel Peace Prize to the Black Madonna.

Size of the icon:
48 × 32½ × 1½ inches/
122.2 × 82.2 × 3.5 cm

Left-hand page: Services are often held outdoors in order to accommodate the vast number of visitors.

Right: The Black Madonna is protected by a silver cover that is removed for special occasions.

The queen of Poland. A succession of miracles is attributed to the icon. When Swedish troops were on the point of launching an assault on Częstochowa in 1655, the Polish army, who were greatly outnumbered, prayed to the Black Madonna and the enemy withdrew. After that, King Jan II Kazimierz (1609–72) crowned Our Lady of Częstochowa "queen of Poland" and made the city the spiritual center of the land. In 1920, Russian troops were building up by the Vistula River for an attack on Warsaw when, on September 15, the Madonna appeared in the clouds above the city and the Russians were beaten, an event that went down in history as the "Miracle of the Vistula."

Under the Nazi occupation of Poland, Hitler prohibited pilgrimages to the Jasna Góra monastery, but many Catholics traveled to the holy place in secret. After the liberation in 1945, more than half a million pilgrims gathered at the shrine of the Madonna; the following year, on September 8, 1946, the number had trebled. Today, the shrine is visited by a continuous stream of visitors.

Below left and right: The faithful on their way to the main destination of their pilgrimage, the Black Madonna.

Sergiyev Posad Monastery

THE MONASTERY OF THE HOLY TRINITY AT SERGIYEV POSAD IS RUSSIA'S MOST FAMOUS
MONASTERY AND THE SPIRITUAL CAPITAL OF RUSSIAN ORTHODOX CHRISTIANS. FOUNDED
IN THE FOURTEENTH CENTURY BY SERGIUS OF RADONEZH, IT HAS PLAYED A DECISIVE
ROLE IN THE DEVELOPMENT OF RUSSIAN ORTHODOX MONASTICISM.

Located some 43 miles/70 km from Moscow, the most important shrine in the Russian Orthodox Church was founded by St. Sergius of Radonezh (1319–92). It was built around a simple wooden church in an isolated spot. Sergius was elected abbot of the monastery in 1355 and was made a patron saint of Russia in 1422. That same year, the Cathedral of the Holy Trinity, which is decorated with magnificent frescoes, was erected over his tomb. Since then, it has been the custom for members of the imperial family and other notables to be baptized and married in the church, and many have also sought refuge here during difficult times. During its long history, the monastery has repeatedly been forced to defend itself against aggressors and plunderers. In the fourteenth century, it was razed by the Tartars, and the Lithuanians, Swedes, and Poles have all attacked at various times. In order to secure the monastery, defensive walls punctuated by eight watchtowers were constructed, which gave it a fortress-like aspect. By the nineteenth century, the monastery at Sergiyev Posad had become Russia's biggest landowner, thanks to its remote location and donations from the Crown. A village (*posad*) grew up outside its walls that gradually developed into the city of Sergiyev Posad (meaning the "settlement of

Sergiyev Posad
Monastery

FACT FILE

1340
Founding of the monastery by Sergius of Radonezh.
1392
Death of St. Sergius, "prior and master of all the monasteries of Russia."
1422–23
Construction of the Cathedral of the Holy Trinity.
1559–85
Construction of the Cathedral of the Assumption.
1608–10
Monastery besieged by Polish troops.
1814
Theological academy established in the palace of the czar.
1920
Dissolution of the monastery.
1993
Inscribed as a UNESCO World Heritage Site.

Below: The architecture of the Cathedral of the Assumption, constructed in the sixteenth century, is based on that of the Cathedral of the Dormition of the Virgin in the Kremlin in Moscow.

Left-hand page: Protected by walls and turrets, the monastery creates a fortress-like impression.

Right: The domes of the Cathedral of the Assumption, with their Oriental-looking star pattern.

Sergius"), whose name was changed to Zagorsk during the Soviet period.

A monastery of the highest rank. In 1744, Czarina Elizabeth I raised the monastery to the status of *lavra*, whose original meaning was "corridor" (referring in this context to the corridor onto which the monks' cells opened). In the Orthodox Church, it is used as an honorary name for a monastery of the highest rank. The conferring of this honor inaugurated a tradition of annual pilgrimages to the monastery by the imperial family. Elizabeth is responsible for the construction of the 289-ft/88-m high bell tower, which remains the tallest church tower in Russia. In front of the tower is a holy well reputed to have healing properties. Pilgrims come by the million to drink its water.

After the Russian Revolution, the monastery was nationalized and closed. Its buildings were transformed into museums housing the most magnificent Orthodox artworks in the world. However, in 1945, Stalin returned the Sergiyev Posad monastery to the Orthodox Church, and on April 16, 1946, a religious service was once again celebrated in the Cathedral of the Holy Trinity. Since 1989, the Russian Orthodox Church has regained much of the importance it enjoyed before the Revolution.

FRANCE

Carnac

CARNAC, IN THE REGION OF BRITTANY, IS HOME TO THE WORLD'S LARGEST, MOST
MYSTERIOUS, AND SEEMINGLY ENDLESS COLLECTION OF MEGALITHS, BEARING
MAGICAL WITNESS TO THE SPIRITUAL LIFE OF A LOST PEOPLE.

O n France's North Atlantic coast stands a prehistoric monument consisting of over three thousand stone monoliths. These menhirs (from the Breton *ar-men-hir*, meaning "long stone") were hewn from granite and either stand alone or are arranged in rows or circles. What is known for certain is that the stones were not erected by the Romans or the Gauls. The sacred monument was created toward the end of the Neolithic period with extraordinary effort by an unknown people in the hope of overcoming death and achieving eternal life.

Over the centuries, the supposed magic of the stones has continually drawn people to them and continues to do so today. In the thirteenth century AD, it was written that on certain holidays some of the menhirs would rotate, and many of the stones are believed to emit plaintive or woeful cries that can be heard when the ear is placed against them. Many believe the stones were created by living beings who possessed the gift of magic and who then endowed the stones with supernatural powers.

Fertility symbols. Until well into the modern age, the stones were revered by the Bretons as cult objects. During earlier epochs, they served religious purposes and were "used" by all the different cultures that

Carnac

FACT FILE

The collection of menhirs in the Brittany region includes far in excess of 3,000 stones. The stones are up to 13 ft/ 4 m high and are aligned in rows about 2 miles/ 3 km long (originally 5 miles/8 km in length). These menhirs date from between 3000 and 1800 BC.

Left-hand page: The prehistoric stone monoliths up to 13 ft/4 m high stand in rows about 2 miles/ 3 km long.

Right: Many researchers regard Carnac as an enormous cemetery because there are also a number of passage graves containing decorated stones; however, the graves are less ancient than the menhirs.

encountered them. The Roman armies came across them during their campaigns and carved images of their gods into them. During the Middle Ages, they were "Christianized" through the addition of crucifixes and other religious symbols, and many were used in the building of churches. At other times during the history of Christianity, however, some of the stones were destroyed, damaged, or buried by priests in order to divest the pagan creations of their power.

Modern visitors are also deeply moved by the stones. Their reactions range from respect for those who erected them to a belief in the power of the stones to promote fertility. Couples wanting to have children have been known to gather at night at this magic place to dance around the stones or anoint them with oil. The Menhir of Saint-Cado in particular is believed to boost the fertility of women.

Below: More than 3,000 menhirs bear mysterious testimony to a vanished civilization that began erecting them over 5,000 years ago.

Cluny Abbey

CLUNY ABBEY WAS THE SOURCE OF NEW IDEAS THAT HAD A PROFOUND IMPACT
ON MEDIEVAL MONASTICISM. THROUGH ITS REFORM OF NUMEROUS OTHER
MONASTERIES, THIS MODEL BENEDICTINE FOUNDATION IN BURGUNDY BECAME
THE CHURCH'S SECOND MOST IMPORTANT SPIRITUAL CENTER AFTER ROME.

Cluny Abbey was founded in AD 910 by the pious Duke William I of Aquitaine (reigned 886–918). William exempted it from all taxation and prohibited any interference in its affairs by the secular authorities. He entrusted the abbey and its estate to St. Peter and placed it under the protection of St. Peter's representative on earth: the pope. This was to have a decisive influence on the future of the monastery. Another key factor in its development was the long period spent in office (a total of 193 years) by its five most famous abbots: Odo, Majolus,

Cluny Abbey

Odilo, Hugues de Semur, and Petrus Venerabilis. It was this continuity and the skillful leadership of these abbots that made Cluny great and powerful.

Around AD 1000, Odilo singled out caring for the spiritual welfare of the faithful as a monk's most important duty: Prayer on behalf of the dead would, he believed, save Christendom from eternal damnation, and consequently, this was practiced with a new intensity at Cluny. In 1098, Pope Urban II gave the abbey the epithet "Light of the World."

The Cluniac model was extremely successful. For a long period of time, the abbey was showered with endowments and oversaw the adoption of the Cluny reforms by

AD 910
Cluny Abbey founded.
1088–1131
Construction of the third
abbey church.
**Fifteenth–eighteenth
centuries**
Many new monastery
buildings erected.
1790
Dissolution of the
monastery.
Up to 1823
Systematic destruction of
the church, which was used
as a quarry.

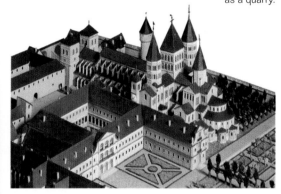

Above: Model of the
monastery in the abbey
museum, showing the
church known as Cluny III.

Right: All that now remains
of Cluny III is the southern
transept and its tower.

Left-hand page: Museum
pieces: a Romanesque altar
table and the eight capitals
from the ambulatory pillars.

many other monasteries. The *Cluniacensis ecclesia*
acquired the status of a Christian elite.

The largest place of worship in the world. Cluny
was unusual for its administration. Normally, monasteries
were independent and connected with other abbeys only
informally or through their monastic order. As more
and more monasteries embraced the Cluniac model,
priors who were answerable to the abbot of Cluny were
put in charge of these houses, and a vast network of
monasteries gradually developed. In 1016, Cluny was
granted additional privileges by the pope, which resulted
in an ever greater number of Benedictine monasteries
adopting the Cluniac reforms. In 1088, work began on
the construction of the third abbey church, which was
largely demolished in the wake of the French Revolution
and survives only in part. With a nave and four aisles, two
transepts, five radiating chapels, numerous towers, and a
length of 614 ft/187 m, "Cluny III" was for centuries the
largest Christian church in the world.

FRANCE

Fontenay Abbey

FONTENAY ABBEY, WHICH DATES FROM THE TWELFTH CENTURY, LIES IN A DENSELY
WOODED VALLEY IN BURGUNDY. PROBABLY THE BEST-PRESERVED MEDIEVAL
CISTERCIAN ABBEY IN THE WORLD, IT WAS FOUNDED BY THE ORDER'S MOST
IMPORTANT FIGURE, BERNARD OF CLAIRVAUX.

Fontenay Abbey

Fontenay Abbey was founded in 1118 by Bernard of Clairvaux on land that was given to him by his uncle. The first Cistercian monks settled at the monastery around 1130. In 1139, the bishop of Norwich (England) fled to Fontenay to escape persecution. He expressed his gratitude by providing the monastery with the means to continue work on the construction of the abbey church, which was eventually consecrated by Pope Eugene III in 1147. By around 1200, the monastery had grown to such an extent that it was now able to accommodate 300 monks, and in 1259 it was declared a royal abbey. Fontenay was badly damaged during the religious wars of the sixteenth century, and in 1790, one year after the beginning of the French Revolution, the last eight monks left the abbey. In 1791, the monastery was secularized and turned into a paper mill. This industrial use ultimately saved the monastic buildings from total destruction.

Bernard of Clairvaux. Bernard of Clairvaux (1090–1153) entered Cîteaux Abbey, which was founded in 1098 and is located south of Dijon (Burgundy), in 1113. Just a few years later, he was sent out from the abbey from which the Cistercian order takes its name to

Left: The monastic complex from the east. On the left is the east wing of the cloister; on the right is the abbey church with transept chapels and choir.

establish Fontenay Abbey (also in Burgundy). He then became its first abbot. The Cistercians saw themselves as a Benedictine reform order. They adopted a stricter, more ascetic approach to monastic life and monastic architecture, and placed a new emphasis on the Benedictine rules composed by St. Benedict of Nursia. Bernard of Clairvaux is often described as the founder of the Cistercians, but the order's founding fathers were in fact Robert de Molesme, Alberic de Cîteaux, and Stephen Harding. St. Bernard is, however, the outstanding figure of the order and its most prominent saint. He is also regarded as one of the most significant figures of the twelfth century.

The abbey church at Fontenay is the oldest surviving Cistercian church in France. The abbey's most beautiful aspect is its simple but delightful cloister. Bernard rejected all forms of church decoration on the basis that it distracted the faithful from their prayer and inner contemplation.

FACT FILE

1118
Fontenay Abbey founded.
1130–47
Construction of the abbey church.
1174
St. Bernard canonized by Pope Alexander III.
1906
Edouard Aynard acquires the monastery site and begins to restore it—a process that takes until the 1990s.
1981
Inscribed as a UNESCO World Heritage Site.
August 20
St. Bernard's feast day.

Below left: Interior of the abbey church—a perfect example of austere Cistercian aesthetics.

Below right: The chapter room—a simple vaulted assembly room of great beauty and quietude.

FRANCE, CONQUES

Sainte-Foy Abbey

DATING FROM THE NINTH CENTURY AD, THE RELICS OF ST. FAITH IN THE ABBEY OF SAINTE-FOY MADE CONQUES IN SOUTHWEST FRANCE ONE OF THE MOST IMPORTANT STOPS ON THE PILGRIMAGE ROUTE TO SANTIAGO DE COMPOSTELA.

At the very time that the hermit Dadon is thought to have built the first church at the place where the Early Romanesque abbey dedicated to the 12-year-old virgin martyr St. Faith was later erected, the relics of St. James were found in Compostela. Pilgrims streamed along Via Podiensis—the French pilgrimage route—to Spain. The stops along the way soon acquired an exalted status themselves and grew wealthy from the gifts of devout pilgrims. At this time, the relics of the martyr St. Faith ("Foy" in French), who was tortured and beheaded around AD 303 under Emperor Diocletian, were kept in Agen Abbey and had made Agen an important place of pilgrimage. Arosnidus, a monk from Conques, lived among the brothers at Agen for ten years before being able to get close enough to the saint's relics to purloin them and take them back with him to Conques, where they have been kept in a golden reliquary statue since the end of the ninth century. The effect of this religious theft was indeed to divert the stream of pilgrims from Agen to Conques and to put Sainte-Foy Abbey on the map as a place of special holiness. Pilgrims and kings donated precious stones to be incorporated into the statue, and Abbot Odolric embarked on the construction of a new

Left-hand page: The tympanum of the Last Judgment above the main door of the church is one of the most important creations of Romanesque sculpture.

Right: The statue of St. Faith once attracted crowds of pilgrims. It is one of the most valuable of all early medieval reliquaries.

Below: Conques. View of the village and abbey church against a charming rural backdrop.

church that was completed in 1120. However, with the dwindling of pilgrim traffic and the advent of religious wars in the sixteenth century, Conques' importance waned and it gradually fell into decline. The monastery was eventually dissolved in 1789 during the French Revolution.

The Last Judgment. Of particular note at this holy place is the great tympanum of the Last Judgment above the main entrance to the abbey church. Created under Abbot Bonifacius between 1107 and 1125, the relief represents storytelling at its most vivid. It features biblical figures and immortalizes specific abbots, kings, and bishops—many of whom are among the damned. At the center sits Christ enthroned, while in the lower section, the archangel Michael and Satan are busy weighing souls. On the right, we see the sinners being cast into hell, while on the left, the righteous are welcomed into heaven by angels. The thieving monk, Arosnidus, stands in the left-hand corner: His misdemeanor was clearly found to be worthy of commemorating in stone.

FRANCE

Mont-Saint-Michel

MONT-SAINT-MICHEL IS A ROCKY ISLET IN THE MUDFLATS OF AVRANCHES OFF THE
NORTH COAST OF FRANCE. THE FORMER BENEDICTINE MONASTERY SITS PROUDLY
ATOP THE ISLAND.

In the sixth century AD, there were two oratories and a handful of hermits on Mont Tombe, as the small island with a diameter of less than ⅔ mile/ 1 km was then known. The tiny community was serviced by a priest from the mainland and was succeeded in the eighth century by the construction of a new monastic complex. According to legend, the archangel Gabriel appeared to Bishop Aubert of Avranches in 708 and instructed him to build a church on the rocky isle. The bishop at first ignored the command, whereupon the angel burned a hole in his skull with his finger. Convinced by this display of force majeure, Aubert began building, and on October 16, 709, the new shrine of St. Michael, which had received relics from Monte Gargano in Italy and had been given a new name—Mont-Saint-Michel—was consecrated. At that time, the causeway to the island was submerged during high tide and could only be reached during low tide. The tide used to come in very quickly and took many lives, thereby increasing the challenging character of the island as a place of pilgrimage.

A reputation that spread far and wide. In 933, the Normans conquered the Cherbourg Peninsula, which put Mont-Saint-Michel on the border of Brittany.

Mont-Saint-Michel

FACT FILE

AD **708**
Construction of the
monastery begins.
1023
Construction of the
Romanesque church begins.
1204
Addition of a Gothic cloister
and refectory.
1789
Abbey transformed into a
prison during the French
Revolution.
1836
Victor Hugo campaigns to
have the island recognized
as an architectural treasure.
1863
Closure of the monastery;
the island declared a
historical monument.
1979
Inscribed as a UNESCO
World Heritage Site.

Left-hand page: View of the mount from the south (mainland). The shrine of St. Michael is one of the most visited places in northern France.

Right: While the Romanesque nave has survived, the choir collapsed in 1421 and was rebuilt between 1446 and 1521 in the Gothic style.

Thanks to generous gifts from Duke Richard II, work was able to start in 1023—under Abbot Hildebert—on a new Romanesque church designed by the Italian architect Guglielmo di Volpiano. The church was aligned east-to-west on the top of the hill. Underground crypts and chapels had to be constructed in order to support the extraordinary architecture.

The west front of the church was built in the twelfth century by Robert de Thorigny, Duke of Normandy, and in 1204, a Gothic cloister and refectory were added through the patronage of King Philip II Augustus of France. The abbey was to inspire the building of numerous other monasteries, including St. Michael's Mount in Cornwall, England. However, with the Reformation, the influence of Mont-Saint-Michel waned, and by the French Revolution, there were hardly any monks left on the island. The abbey was closed and transformed into a prison. Today, the pilgrims of yore have been replaced by crowds of tourists.

Below: The cloister was completed in 1228. It has double rows of syncopated arcading.

FRANCE, CHARTRES

Notre-Dame Cathedral in Chartres

A NUMBER OF CHURCHES LATER DESTROYED BY FIRE HAD PREVIOUSLY STOOD ON
THE SPOT WHERE, IN 1094, WORK BEGAN ON ONE OF THE WORLD'S MOST SPLENDID
GOTHIC CATHEDRALS: NOTRE-DAME IN CHARTRES.

Chartres, on the Eure River, is only 56 miles/90 km from Paris. In the middle of the town is a hill that is thought to have been a center of cult activity even in pre-Christian times. Numerous legends were invented in order to underpin the significance of the place. What is certain is that the site was occupied almost continually from the ninth century AD onward by the cathedral's predecessor churches. The cathedral in its current form dates mainly from the twelfth and thirteenth centuries. Only parts of the west front survived the fire of 1194. At the time, the catastrophe was seen as a sign

from the Virgin Mary that an even bigger and more splendid church should be built in order to provide the cathedral's main relic—the tunic Mary is supposed to have worn during the birth of Jesus—with a worthy home.

The miracle of Mary's tunic. After the fire of 1194, a legend was begun that reinforced popular belief in the Mother of God to work miracles. All attempts to put out the flames had failed, and the village and church were more or less completely destroyed. However, the tunic donated by Charlemagne's grandson in 876 was found unscathed in the crypt several days later.

Chartres as a model cathedral. The extraordinary size and clarity of design of the Chartres cathedral made

Notre-Dame
Cathedral

Left-hand page: Notre-Dame towers above the surrounding buildings. Visitors to Chartres are greeted by majestic views of the cathedral from miles around.

Right: The cathedral's rose windows are among the most beautiful and precious sights in all of Gothic architecture—which by no means lacks in aesthetic appeal.

FACT FILE

Notre-Dame Cathedral in Chartres contains the largest crypt of any French cathedral. Vendôme Chapel houses the tunic of the Virgin Mary. The structure has 172 windows with a total area of approximately 28,000 sq ft/ 2,600 sq m.
Length: 427 ft/130.2 m
Height of the nave: 123 ft/37.5 m
Height of the towers: 338 ft/103 m and 367 ft/112 m
Date of construction: 1194–1220
1979
Inscribed as a UNESCO World Heritage Site.

it a model for numerous later churches. The stained-glass windows bathe the interior in a mysterious blue light. The cathedral's windows, together with the windows of the cathedral in Bourges, France, constitute one of the most important collections of stained glass in the world.

Equally remarkable is the cathedral's architectural sculpture. The history of monumental sculpture in France began with the cathedral's three closely positioned west doors. After Notre-Dame in Paris, Notre-Dame Cathedral in Chartres is France's most famous cathedral. In addition to the building's art-historical importance, another reason for its popularity is that many of the people who come here feel the cathedral to be a place of palpable holiness and great spirituality.

Above: The sturdy buttressing of the outer walls allows them to be pierced by large windows.

Right: View of the cathedral's lofty interior, looking east down the single-aisled nave.

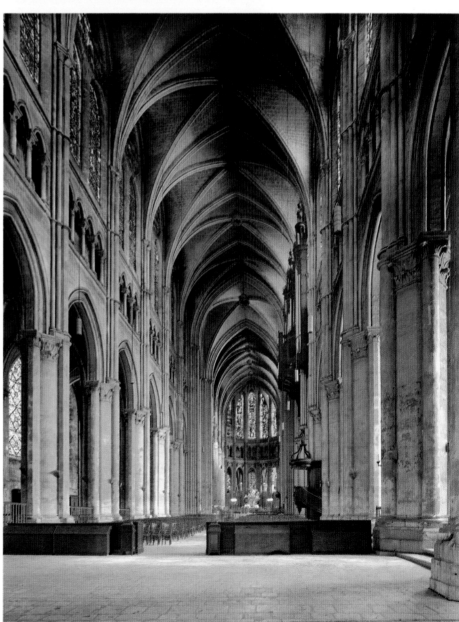

FRANCE

Lourdes

IN 1858, THE VIRGIN MARY APPEARED TO 14-YEAR-OLD BERNADETTE SOUBIROUS
ABOVE A BLOOMING ROSE BUSH. THE APPARITION LEFT BEHIND A SIGN OF HER
LOVE IN THE FORM OF A SPRING WITH HEALING PROPERTIES.

From 1830 onward, reports of apparitions of the Virgin Mary multiplied. This was interpreted by the Catholic Church as Mary appearing to her children who had strayed from the path of faith. On February 11, 1858, Mary appeared in Lourdes and left a sign of her healing power. On the spot where she appeared, a spring burst forth that turned Lourdes into a place of miraculous healing. The Lourdes spring is world-famous, and countless letters attest to its healing powers. Mary appeared here a total of 18 times—more times than ever before or since in the history of Marian apparitions. On her fourth apparition, she told Bernadette Soubirous the following: "Do me the favor of coming to me 14 days in a row and I promise to make you happy. Not in this world but in the next." During the course of her apparitions, Mary told the girl a host of secrets that Bernadette took with her to her grave, having been made to promise not to divulge them.

Bernadette Soubirous. Bernadette Soubirous died on April 16, 1879, at the age of 35, and was buried in the chapel of St. Joseph in Nevers, France. When her casket was opened in 1908, Bernadette's corpse was found to be unchanged, looking as it had when she died: the veins in

Lourdes

FACT FILE

February 11
Feast of Our Lady
of Lourdes.
Cures
Eighty percent of those
cured are women. More
than 7,000 medically
conspicuous cures have
been documented to date,
and some 2,000 of them
have been classified by
doctors as inexplicable.
Following thorough
investigation, 68 have been
recognized by the Catholic
Church as miracle cures.
The most recent was that of
multiple sclerosis sufferer
Jean-Pierre Bély in 1987.

Left-hand page: The small town of Lourdes, located in the foothills of the Pyrenees and south of Tarbes, fills up with pilgrims at regular intervals.

Right: A statue of the Virgin Mary in a grotto serves as a reminder of the miracle of the apparitions of Our Lady of Lourdes here in the nineteenth century that made the town famous throughout the world.

her forearms had a bluish tinge and protruded slightly, her fingernails were pink and unblemished, and her face was tanned. In 1919, her casket was opened again and still she showed no signs of decay, looking almost as she had in 1908. Her face and hands were coated with a film of wax and her body was put on display in a shrine in the chapel of her convent in Nevers. In 1933, Bernadette was canonized by Pope Pius XI.

During the years that followed the apparitions, Lourdes developed into one of the Catholic Church's holiest places of pilgrimage, and millions of pilgrims now come here in the hope of finding relief from their ailments at the holy spring. The first cure occurred in 1858 when Catherine Latapie Chourat withdrew her paralyzed arm from the water to find it had been healed.

Below: The holy water and healing grace of the Mother of God are the last hope for many of the sick who undergo the rigors of traveling to Lourdes.

Santiago de Compostela

THE ROMANS NAMED THE NORTHWEST COAST OF GALICIA IN SPAIN FINISTERRE, MEANING "LAND'S END." NEARBY, A CHURCH WAS RAISED OVER WHAT IS PRESUMED TO BE THE TOMB OF ST. JAMES. THIS CHURCH BECAME THE DESTINATION OF ONE OF THE MOST IMPORTANT PILGRIMAGE ROUTES IN THE WORLD.

For over a thousand years, pilgrims from every corner of Europe have been traveling along the Way of St. James to the Cathedral of Santiago de Compostela, which was built over the tomb of the apostle St. James. According to legend, St. James returned to Jerusalem from Spain, following a successful period spent as a missionary, only to be imprisoned by Herod as a Christian and beheaded. His disciples put his body in a boat, and with the help of angels, he was brought back to Spain, where he was buried. This translation of the saint's relics

is documented in Latin texts dating from the seventh century. A more detailed account is given in the famous pilgrim's guide, *Liber Sancti Jacobi*, from the mid-twelfth century, according to which a bright light drew attention to the forgotten grave, leading to its rediscovery around AD 800. Charlemagne is named as the first pilgrim to Santiago. The king of the Franks is also associated with the early campaigns to drive the Moors out of Spain, and St. James is often portrayed on a white horse leading the heavenly hosts into battle against the Moors.

The Way of St. James. Doubts have repeatedly been cast on the legend of St. James. However, this has not prevented Santiago (as St. James is known in

Santiago de Compostela

FACT FILE

AD **899**
Consecration of a basilica
over the tomb of
St. James.
997
Destruction of the basilica
by the Saracens.
1077
Rebuilding of the
destroyed church.
1211
Consecration of the
completed church.
1738
Addition of Baroque facade.
1985
Inscribed as a UNESCO
World Heritage Site.

Above left and right: After their long journey, the pilgrims enter their destination through the impressive Pórtico de la Gloria, the Romanesque entrance sculpted by Master Mateo. Many of the church's doors feature detailed sculptural decoration that also served the purpose of moral instruction.

Spanish) from becoming the third most holy place of pilgrimage in the Catholic Church after Rome and Jerusalem. The Camino de Santiago, the pilgrim's way that leads there, is famous throughout the world. It is undertaken by pilgrims of all religions, who walk the 500 miles/800 km (approximately) to Santiago de Compostela with staff, hat, and scallop shell—the attribute of the saint—from Roncesvalles on the French border, high up in the Pyrenees.

Whenever the saint's feast day (July 25) falls on a Sunday, that year is known as a "holy year." After a lengthy period of privation, the pilgrims enter the cathedral through the impressive Romanesque entrance known as the Pórtico de la Gloria. At the end of a special pilgrims' service, they witness the spectacle of the *botafumeiro* (an enormous censer) being hauled high up into the vault at the end of a rope some 100 ft/30 m long by eight men, swinging backward and forward as it goes. In Santiago, the Holy Spirit is experienced with all the senses.

Left-hand page: The cathedral of Santiago de Compostela with the Raxoi Palace in the foreground.

Right: The facade of the cathedral was rebuilt in 1738 in Spanish Baroque style. The sculptural decoration extends to the very top of the towers.

Montserrat Monastery

THE WOODEN STATUE OF THE BLACK MADONNA IN THE MONASTERY AT
MONTSERRAT, WHICH IS LOCATED AMONG EXTRAORDINARY ROCK FORMATIONS
AT A HEIGHT OF OVER 2,000 FT/600 M, IS KNOWN TO THE SPANISH AS
"LA MORENETA."

Montserrat
Monastery

Ever since the thirteenth century, the monastery at Montserrat, not far from Barcelona, has been attracting pilgrims from all over the world. Today, as many as three million visitors a year find their way up the rugged mountain to the shrine. They come to see, pass beneath, and pray before the small Romanesque statue of the Black Madonna, which has been dated to the end of the twelfth century. The statue's black coloration is the result of the darkening of the various coats of varnish it has been given over the course of time. According to the Catholic tradition, the figure of the Virgin Mary was carved by St. Luke the Evangelist around AD 50, and during the years of Moorish rule of the Iberian Peninsula, it was hidden in the Santa Cova (meaning "holy grotto"), where it was only rediscovered in 880. According to one legend dating from the thirteenth century, the figure was found by shepherds who were led to the cave by a bright light and heavenly music. The bishop of Manresa, a city on the other side of the mountains, wanted to have the statue brought to him there, but it proved too heavy for any means of transport and could not even be lifted. The Catholic Church interpreted this as the express wish of the Virgin Mary to remain in Montserrat and be venerated there.

FACT FILE

1015
First mention of a church at the time of Oliba, abbot of Ripoll and bishop of Vic.
1592
Consecration of the large basilica at Montserrat.
Nineteenth century
Monastery almost completely destroyed during the Napoleonic Wars.
1881
Pope Leo XIII proclaims the Black Madonna of Montserrat patron saint of Catalonia.

Left-hand page: The rocks around Montserrat offer an ideal place of retreat for hermits, and, indeed, the origins of the monastery go back to the early Middle Ages and the eremitic way of life.

Right: The stories concerning the origins of the Black Madonna of Montserrat go back to the first century AD. However, it is known to have been made in the late twelfth century.

Below: From the monastery at 2,362 ft/ 720 m, a number of routes lead up to Sant Jeroni, the highest peak in the sandstone range at 4,055 ft/1,236 m.

Pilgrims from all over the world. In the ninth century, there were four chapels on Montserrat, just one of which—dedicated to San Acisclo—survives today. It is also known that a Benedictine monastery of Santa Cecília existed as early as 899. This was initially a daughter foundation of the Benedictine abbey at Ripoll. However, most visitors are interested in this place not because of its monastic history but because of the Black Madonna. Many miracles that have occurred in these mountains have been attributed to her, and a number of mission churches were also dedicated to her in the New World—notably in Mexico, Chile, and Peru. The list of those who have made the pilgrimage to Montserrat includes a number of popes and saints, including St. Ignatius of Loyola, who wrote his *Spiritual Exercises* here. The monastery was expanded in the eighteenth century when the pilgrim traffic exceeded its capacity. Today, some 80 monks still live here and venerate the Virgin in the basilica.

Fátima

IN 1917, DURING WORLD WAR I, THE MADONNA APPEARED TO THREE SHEPHERD CHILDREN IN NORTHERN PORTUGAL. OVER THE FOLLOWING MONTHS, SHE REAPPEARED ON THE THIRTEENTH DAY OF EACH MONTH.

On May 13, 1917, the Virgin Mary appeared to three shepherd children above a holm oak in the vicinity of the Portuguese village of Fátima. The children saw a flash of light and then Mary appeared, shining even brighter than the light. According to the children, she wore a dress of the purest white with a cloak of gold covering her head and body, and she held in her hands a rosary of white pearls. Lúcia dos Santos, the eldest of the children at ten years old, said later, "She was barely more than one meter [just over 3 ft] tall and around 18 years old." The

Virgin spoke to Lúcia and was heard by Jacinta Marto but not by Jacinta's brother, Francisco. The Virgin asked the children to come to the same place—the Cova da Iria just outside the village—on the 13th of each month. Her message was the same on each occasion: "Pray, pray, pray, be repentant and ask for forgiveness for your sins." Each month, more people gathered at the site of the apparitions to witness the holy event, and on October 13, 1917, over 70,000 people were present and saw the sun, which was high in the sky, begin to turn like an enormous fire wheel.

In 1927, Lúcia dos Santos was given divine permission to divulge the first two so-called secrets she had been

Fátima

Left-hand page and right: The number of visitors to Fátima on important occasions, such as a papal visit, routinely exceeds the site's capacity, despite the enormous dimensions of the church and forecourt. Pope John Paul II visited Fátima on three occasions and had a special attachment to the place.

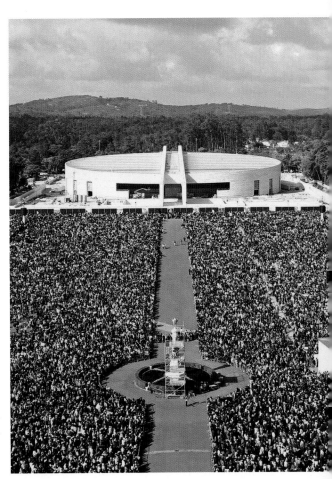

given, which predicted World War II and the rise and fall of Russian communism. She wrote the third secret down in 1942, but it was not revealed until 2000. It told of the assassination of the pope and other Church dignitaries below a cross. It is interesting to note that after surviving the assassination attempt of May 13, 1981, Pope John Paul II credited Our Lady of Fátima—whose first appearance had been on the same day of the year—with saving his life.

The Church of the Most Holy Trinity. On October 13, 2007, the ninetieth anniversary of the Miracle of the Sun, a new church was consecrated in the "Arena of Faith," as the pilgrimage center is known in Church circles. One of the largest churches in the world, the Church of the Most Holy Trinity was designed by the Greek architect Alexander Tombazis. It has a diameter of 410 ft/125 m and can accommodate a congregation of more than 8,000. Today, Fátima is one of the most visited places of pilgrimage in the world.

Below: In thanks for his survival, Pope John Paul II donated to Fátima the bullet that got lodged in his body during the assassination attempt. It has been set into the Madonna's crown.

ITALY

Assisi

ASSISI IS A PICTURESQUE TOWN NESTLED AMONG THE UMBRIAN MOUNTAINS SOME
1,300 FT/400 M ABOVE SEA LEVEL. IT IS THE BIRTHPLACE OF ST. FRANCIS OF ASSISI,
FOUNDER OF THE FRANCISCAN ORDER, PATRON SAINT OF ITALY, AND ONE OF THE
MOST POPULAR SAINTS IN THE HISTORY OF THE CATHOLIC CHURCH.

St. Francis, whose real name was Giovanni Bernardone, was the son of a prosperous merchant. After experiencing an epiphany at the age of 24 when, during Mass one day, he heard the voice of St. Matthew the Evangelist telling him to go out into the world, renounce all possessions, and do good works, he traveled through Italy preaching poverty. During 1209–10, he and 12 apostles founded the Order of Friars Minor. In 1212, Clare of Assisi joined the order, also wishing to lead a life of compassion and poverty. Together, Clare and Francis founded the

order of Poor Clares at San Damiano outside Assisi as a female branch of the Franciscan order. Clare of Assisi was canonized after her death. Francis composed a rule for his order, based on the Gospels, which was eventually approved by Pope Honorius III in 1223, albeit with a toned-down version of the radical poverty demanded by St. Francis. In 1224, while living as a hermit in the mountains, Francis had a vision and received the stigmata—the sign of Christ's five wounds—on his body, thereby becoming the earliest recorded Christian stigmatic. However, St. Francis never showed the marks to anyone, and they were only discovered after his death in 1226. There are many legends connected with this popular saint.

Left-hand page: San Francesco in Assisi. The remains of St. Francis were brought to the Lower Church in 1230 and buried under the high altar. Given his ideal of poverty, a less grandiose resting place might have been more appropriate.

A holy place of pilgrimage. Assisi, with its 3,000 or so inhabitants, has been one of Italy's most important places of pilgrimage for centuries. The Basilica di San Francesco, where the saint's relics are kept, attracts millions of Christian pilgrims and art lovers every year, not least because the frescoes by Giotto and other artists depicting St. Francis's life story make the basilica one of Italy's most attractive churches. Francis was canonized on July 6, 1228, and Pope Gregory IX laid the foundation stone of the church the very next day. St. Francis's remains were translated to the church in 1230. He was reburied swiftly and under conditions of the utmost secrecy in order to prevent the theft of his relics. His remains, which had been buried under the high altar, were not discovered until 1818, when his skeleton was found to be fully intact. In 1997, Assisi was hit by an earthquake. The roof of the church collapsed, killing four people. The famous frescoes were damaged, but have been restored and were put back on display in all their former glory just two years later.

FACT FILE

1181
Birth of Giovanni Bernardone, known as Francesco.
1204
St. Francis is taken prisoner during the war with Perugia.
1214–15
St. Francis travels in Italy, France, and Spain.
1219
St. Francis takes part in the Fifth Crusade and travels to Egypt.
1226
Death of St. Francis on October 3.
2000
Inscribed as a UNESCO World Heritage Site.

Right and above: The Upper Church contains the famous frescoes depicting scenes from the saint's life, including the dramatic domestic episode in which St. Francis hands his father his clothes and dissociates himself from him for good.

ITALY

Santa Maria Novella

THIS WAS ONCE THE PRINCIPAL CHURCH OF THE DOMINICANS, THE ORDER OF
FRIAR-PREACHERS, IN FLORENCE. THE MESSAGE CONVEYED THROUGH THE SPOKEN
WORD FROM THE PULPIT AND THROUGH THE EXQUISITE FRESCOES BY CELEBRATED
PAINTERS WAS ONE OF ADMONITION, SOLACE, AND SALVATION.

Today, the church of Santa Maria Novella in Florence is visited primarily for its art. Its Renaissance facade by the great theoretician of art and architecture, Leon Battista Alberti, is regarded as the cradle of world architecture, and its famous *Holy Trinity* fresco by Masaccio is considered one of the inaugural works of Renaissance painting. The church is actually a medieval building, and in its spaciousness and flat surfaces represents a fine example of Italian Gothic. It was once the domain of the Dominicans, who used to preach here to large congregations.

Santa Maria Novella

The intellectualism of the Dominicans. Unlike the Franciscans, the Dominicans, from the very beginning, were an order of clerics. Their founder, St. Dominic (1170–1221), had traveled far and wide preaching against heretics—in particular, the Cathars of southern France. In 1215, in Toulouse, France, he founded the first clerical convent with a small band of helpers. Realizing how important education and rhetorical skills were for preachers, he sent his Toulouse brothers to study and establish further communities in Paris, and chose to establish a new center himself in the university city of Bologna, Italy. During St. Dominic's time, the discussion and interpretation of doctrine was taking place more and

Right: A cradle of world architecture: Leon Battista Alberti's new facade, for the medieval church, begun in 1458.

more at the major theological schools. For this reason, his brother preachers not only had to be extremely well educated, but they also had to be based in the centers of intellectual debate. The community of Dominicans in Florence was established by Dominican brothers from Bologna.

The path to salvation. The claim the Dominicans made for their work is clearly expressed in Andrea Bonaiuti's 1367 fresco *Triumph of the Church* in what is now known as the Spanish Chapel (formerly the convent's chapter room). It depicts the path to salvation that can assure people of a place in heaven if only they allow themselves to be guided by the Dominicans, who feature importantly in various parts of the painting, preaching and pointing out the path of righteousness.

Below: Santa Maria Novella is one of the largest churches of the mendicant orders. This spacious hall enabled the Dominicans to preach to large congregations.

FACT FILE

Length of the church:
Approximately 330 ft/100 m
1246
Start of construction.
1360
Building completed by the Dominican Jacopo Talenti.
1365–97
Frescoes painted in the Spanish Chapel by Andrea Bonaiuti (Andrea da Firenze).
1425–28
Holy Trinity fresco by Masaccio.
From 1458
Facade remodeled by Leon Battista Alberti.
Fifteenth century
Additional frescoes by Domenico Ghirlandaio and Filippino Lippi.
1982
City of Florence inscribed as a UNESCO World Heritage Site.

The Vatican and St. Peter's Basilica

"YOU ARE THE ROCK UPON WHICH I WILL BUILD MY CHURCH!" SAID JESUS TO
ST. PETER. TODAY, ST. PETER'S BASILICA, ONE OF THE CATHOLIC CHURCH'S HOLIEST
SITES, STANDS ON THE PLACE WHERE ST. PETER WAS BURIED.

St. Peter's
Basilica

In the Orthodox, Roman Catholic, and Anglican Churches, Christ's disciple Peter is venerated as a saint and the first bishop of Rome. For the Catholic Church, the "Petrine principle," as expressed through Christ's own words, also forms the basis for the supreme authority of the pope over the entire Church.

The Vatican, located within the city of Rome, is the smallest sovereign state in the world. Its head and absolute monarch is the pope. The most important building in this tiny state is St. Peter's Basilica, which sits in majesty at its center.

This state, ruled by the popes, has just 550 citizens, whose citizenship is linked to a specific function or office and is valid for a restricted period of time. A further 3,000 people work in the Vatican as staff members and officials. The state is protected by the Swiss Guard, the papal army sometimes referred to as the smallest army in the world. However, the popes have not always resided here on the *mons vaticanus* on the right bank of the Tiber River, where Emperor Nero built his circus. Starting in 1378, the papacy experienced one of the various low points in its history with the Great Schism in the Latin Church, which lasted until 1417. During this time, there were two popes—one in Avignon, France, and one in Rome.

A place of martyrdom. The dome of St. Peter's, the center of the Roman Catholic world, soars 433 ft/132 m above the city. The basilica is the work of some of the most famous architects of the Renaissance—most notably, Michelangelo. Following the ancient custom of using older buildings as a quarry, the stone was taken from the Colosseum and the Forum Romanum, and the marble slabs from ruined Roman temples. The colonnades around the Egyptian obelisk were designed by Gian Lorenzo Bernini in the mid-sixteenth century. From a Catholic point of view, the obelisk stands on blood-soaked ground. In Nero's day, when those of different religious views were tortured and executed, many a martyr was created on this spot. The victims included Christians, one of whom was St. Peter, the "rock" on which, over the course of 2,000 years, the world's biggest empire of faith has been built.

Above: View of St. Peter's Square (encompassed by imposing colonnades) in front of St. Peter's Basilica and the living quarters of the popes.

Above right: St. Peter's Basilica with its dome by Michelangelo and facade by Carlo Maderno. The rebuilding of the church took about a century.

Right: Interior of St. Peter's, showing Gian Lorenzo Bernini's *Baldacchino* (1624–33). The Chair of St. Peter can be seen in the background.

ITALY

Santa Casa di Loreto

EVER SINCE THE MIDDLE AGES, THE HOLY HOUSE OF LORETO HAS BEEN ONE OF
THE WORLD'S MOST POPULAR MARIAN SHRINES. IT IS VISITED BY FOUR MILLION
CHRISTIAN PILGRIMS EACH YEAR.

According to the New Testament, Jesus was brought up by his mother, Mary, and his father, Joseph, in the house where his mother was born in the small town of Nazareth. Three hundred years after the death of Christ, Roman emperor Constantine (circa AD 280–337), who had converted to Christianity, built a basilica around the house, creating one of the largest shrines in the Catholic Church.

During the Crusades, the Holy House was endangered and, according to Catholic legend, was transported to present-day Croatia by angels in 1291. In Nazareth

there was an empty space, while in Croatia the house suddenly appeared in a bare field. The village priest was brought to the place by shepherds and had a vision of the Virgin Mary in which she revealed to him that this had been her house in Nazareth. On December 20, 1294, the building was moved by angels for a second time when the area was invaded by Muslim warriors. After remaining for a short time in Recanati, Italy, it was moved to its current resting place in Loreto. Since that time, it has been known as Santa Casa di Loreto and has been revered as one of the Catholic Church's most important shrines. It is visited by millions of pilgrims each year, and countless miracles and cures are reported to have occurred here.

Santa Casa di Loreto

1469
Construction of a
basilica over the Santa
Casa di Loreto.
1507
Construction of a marble
enclosure around the Santa
Casa within the basilica.
1510
Santa Casa di Loreto
declared a holy place
of pilgrimage.
1910
Based on the story of the
transportation by angels of
the Holy House, Our Lady
of Loreto is declared the
patron saint of pilots.
December 10
Feast day of
Our Lady of Loreto.

Left-hand page: During the
fourteenth century, Loreto
developed into one of Italy's
most important places of
Marian pilgrimage. In 1469,
work started on the
construction of a
new basilica.

Disputed authenticity. The authenticity of the
Santa Casa has long been disputed. Some experts have
demonstrated that the building materials are identical
with those used in Nazareth and pointed out that the
house has no recognizable foundations; while on the other
hand, there is no documentary evidence that the house
ever existed in Nazareth and no reports of such a house
having disappeared. The house was first mentioned in
the fifteenth century; prior to this, there are no historical
records of the existence of the house, even in Italy. The
simplest explanation, and the one accepted by many
Catholics, is that pilgrims brought back the remains
of the house with them to Loreto from Nazareth to be
adored as a relic. The altar on the east wall of the Santa
Casa today bears the Latin inscription "Hic verbum caro
factum est" ("Here was the word made flesh"). The Santa
Casa was given its richly sculpted marble enclosure
during the Renaissance period.

Right and above right: In 1513, Andrea Sansovino was
placed in charge of the building works at Loreto.
He concentrated on the sculptural decoration of the
Santa Casa's marble enclosure, creating numerous figures
and reliefs with the help of various other artists.

Knossos

DURING THE BRONZE AGE, KNOSSOS WAS THE RELIGIOUS AND POLITICAL CENTER
OF THE MINOAN CULTURE OF CRETE—THE KINGDOM OF KING MINOS—AND THE
CEREMONIAL CENTER OF THE BULL CULT. IN THE LEGEND OF THE MINOTAUR, THE
BULL, AN ATTRIBUTE OF THE DIVINE, ASSUMES THE FORM OF A DEMON.

The first signs of human habitation at Knossos go back to 7000 BC. During the nineteenth to sixteenth centuries BC, Knossos grew in phases into a monumental city and the administrative and religious center of the Minoan Empire. During the second millennium BC, an enormous palace complex was developed, with piped water, baths, and over 800 rooms. Knossos and the surrounding area were home to some 80,000 people, and Crete possessed the largest fleet in the Mediterranean.

At the beginning of the seventeenth century BC, a volcanic eruption buried the city under more than 3 ft/1 m of ash. However, because no human skeletons have been found during the course of excavations, it is assumed that the inhabitants had time to flee. As a result of the eruption, the sky remained dark for a long period of time, resulting in climatic changes. During subsequent centuries, further catastrophes, such as earthquakes and tidal waves, hastened the decline of Cretan civilization. By 1450 BC, Crete had become so depleted that it was unable to defend itself against the attacking Mycenaeans, and thus the Minoan era drew to a close.

The Minotaur. Knossos was the center of the bull cult. According to the myth, Zeus fell in love with

The palace at Knossos had up to five stories and over 800 rooms. The built-up areas are known to have covered at least 226,000 sq ft/21,000 sq m on a site of nearly 5½ acres/2.2 ha.

7000 BC
First human habitation

1628 BC
Destruction of Knossos by a volcanic eruption on the island of Santorini in the Cyclades.

1878
Discovery of Knossos by Greek amateur archaeologist Minos Kalokairinos.

1886
Archaeologist Heinrich Schliemann visits the site.

Left-hand page: Surviving parts of the ancient palace complex dating from the Minoan era.

Below: Sculpture of a bull's head in the Heraklion Archaeological Museum (Crete, 1700–1400 BC, marble and gold).

Right: Drawing of the throne room with painted walls and ceiling as it would probably have appeared around 1900 BC.

Europa, the daughter of the Phoenician king, Agenor. In order to avoid being caught by Hera, his wife, Zeus transformed himself into a bull and abducted Europa to Crete. Zeus and Europa had three children: Minos, Rhadamanthys, and Sarpedon.

The family was unable to escape its taurine past, however. Minos, who developed into a cruel ruler of the island, incurred the wrath of Zeus by selfishly keeping Poseidon's gift of a white bull that was intended as a sacrificial offering to Zeus. Zeus punished Minos by awakening in Pasiphaë—Minos's wife—a sexual longing for the bull. Pasiphaë eventually gave birth to the Minotaur, a creature with the body of a man and the head of a bull, who required human sacrifices. To satisfy the Minotaur, Minos fed it seven virgins and seven young men, taken from the Athenians each year by way of tribute for his own son, who had died in Attica. Minos kept the Minotaur hidden in the legendary labyrinth built by Icarus and Daedalus.

Only the brave Athenian, Theseus, who was able to make his way into the labyrinth and out again—thanks to the famous thread of Ariadne, daughter of Minos and Pasiphaë—was able to slaughter the Minotaur and put an end to the toll of sacrificial victims.

Below: Drawing of a model of the extensive ancient complex with an almost modern appearance.

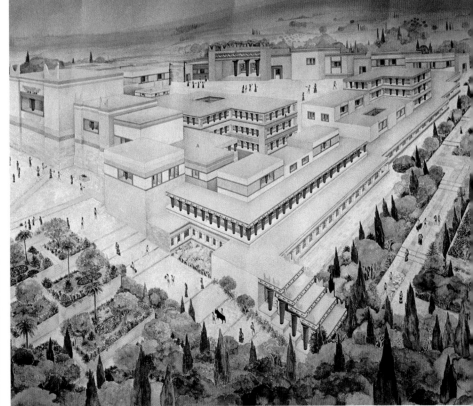

GREECE

Delphi

THE ORACLE OF THE GOD APOLLO, THE MOST IMPORTANT SANCTUARY IN ANCIENT
GREECE, IS SET IN THE MIDDLE OF BREATHTAKINGLY BEAUTIFUL SCENERY AND IS
SURROUNDED BY VARIOUS OTHER COMPLEXES AND TEMPLES.

For the Greeks, Delphi was the center of the world. According to Greek mythology, Zeus released two eagles from opposite ends of the earth and they met over Delphi. Their beaks became entangled and they fell to the earth. The spot was marked by the Omphalos (literally, "navel"), a phallic stone underneath which the grave of Dionysius is supposed to be located. The Castalian Spring, the oracle's most sacred spot, was originally guarded by a feathered dragon called Python, the son of the pre-Hellenic earth goddess Gaia. The name Delphi is derived from the Greek

δελΦός (delphos), meaning the womb or place of birth of the world.

The sacred oracle. Excavations have revealed that this place was inhabited as early as the fifteenth century BC, but according to the poet Homer, it was Apollo himself who brought the oracle to Delphi. As a place of pilgrimage, Delphi attracted visitors from across the entire Greek world. These visitors sought the advice of the oracle on all life's important matters. After receiving a sacrificial offering, the Pythia, a seer specially educated for the role, would make cryptic pronouncements in answer to supplicants' questions, acting as the medium of Apollo. She delivered these pronouncements in the *adyton*, a small room in the Temple of Apollo to which she alone had access. Her answers were then translated by a priest.

The Pythian Games. The Temple of Apollo in its current form dates from the fourth century BC. It was preceded by two earlier temples, of which the first burned down in 548 BC and the second was destroyed in an earthquake. A 5,000-seat theater was also constructed in the fourth century BC where the Pythian Games, the most important games in Greece after the Olympic Games, were held every four years. Originally, there was just one contest: singing to the kithara, a stringed instrument. Sporting competitions were added later.

After Christianity was adopted as the national religion of Byzantium, Emperor Theodosius I closed down the sacred oracle of Apollo in AD 393 and outlawed oracles there as an unacceptable pagan custom. Christianity recognizes no other god but God (the Holy Trinity is merely an abstract relic of earlier polytheism), and from this time forward, the monotheistic principle would rule supreme in Europe.

FACT FILE

Eighth century BC onward
Worship of Apollo.
330 BC
Re-erected Temple of Apollo completed.
191 BC
Conquest by the Romans.
AD 393
Closure of the oracle by Emperor Theodosius I.
1893
Discovery by French archaeologists.
1987
Inscribed as a UNESCO World Heritage Site.

The Delphi Festival, consisting of performances of ancient Greek plays and works inspired by Greek drama, is held each June.

Right: Circular Temple of Athena. Greek ruins, in particular columns but also sculptures that have survived as mere torsos, have inspired architects and artists throughout the ages to reconstruct imaginatively how the original structures would have once looked.

The Parthenon, Acropolis

THE PARTHENON TEMPLE IN ATHENS, THE SANCTUARY OF THE CITY'S PATRON
GODDESS, ATHENA, IS ANCIENT GREECE'S BEST-KNOWN BUILDING. OVER THE
COURSE OF ITS LONG HISTORY, IT HAS BEEN A TEMPLE, A TREASURE CHAMBER,
A FORTRESS, A CHURCH, AND A MOSQUE.

The Parthenon, which perches on the highest point of the Acropolis, has watched over the city of Athens for nearly 2,500 years. It was built in order to give thanks to Athena for saving the city during the Persian Wars. The abbreviated name used today is derived from the Greek *parthenos*, meaning "virgin," and the full name of the sanctuary is the "Temple of Athena the Virgin."

Construction of the temple, under architects Iktinos and Kallikrates and the famous sculptor Phidias (480–430 BC), began in 447 BC on the site where an earlier temple had stood before it was destroyed by the Persians. The guiding light behind the building of the Parthenon was Pericles (495–429 BC), the most influential politician of the day. The purpose of the structure was to house a colossal statue of Athena, a masterpiece by Phidias, in an inner sanctum known as the *cella*. Made of ivory and gold, this statue sadly no longer exists, but we know what it looked like from images on reliefs, vases, and coins. As the most important temple in ancient Greece, the Parthenon served as a shrine for nearly 1,000 years. In the fifth century AD—by which time Athens had declined to the status of a mere provincial city within the Roman Empire—the famous statue had been taken to

The Parthenon, Acropolis

FACT FILE

The Parthenon is a Doric temple with Ionic friezes; it has 17 Doric columns along each side and eight Doric columns on each end. The biggest cost involved in the construction of the Parthenon was that of transporting the stone from Mount Pentelicus, 10 miles/ 16 km away.
Length: 228 ft/69.5 m
Width: 101 ft/30.9 m
Height: 34 ft/10.4 m
1837
Initial excavations.
1987
Inscribed as a UNESCO World Heritage Site.

Below: View of the Parthenon's interior. Restoration work has been underway since 1975.

Left-hand page: The Acropolis, with the large Parthenon temple. Dating mainly from the fifth century BC, the complex is the most important ensemble of ancient Greek architecture.

Right: Standing in "eternal" adoration by the tomb of the king, the famous caryatids of the porch of the Erechtheion on the Acropolis embody the classical ideal of beauty.

Constantinople, where it was probably destroyed during the plundering of the city by Crusaders during the Fourth Crusade (1202–04).

A turbulent history. At the beginning of the thirteenth century, the Parthenon was transformed into a church dedicated to the Virgin Mary. The walls of the cella were dismantled and used in the construction of an apse; most of the sculptures were removed, and those depicting pagan gods were destroyed. In 1456, Athens fell to the Ottomans, and the Parthenon was turned into a mosque. A minaret was added, but otherwise, no damage was done. It had never been a Muslim practice to destroy temples willfully. In travel journals of the seventeenth century, the temple is described as being almost completely intact.

The Parthenon suffered its worst damage during the Venetian bombardment of Athens. The Ottomans were using it as an ordnance depot when it was hit by a shell. The resulting explosion caused serious damage to the building, and the temple has remained in ruins ever since. From 1801 onward, artworks and sculptures were removed and presented to the British Museum in London, where they remain today.

GREECE

The Monasteries of Athos

HÁGION ÓROS ("HOLY MOUNTAIN") IS THE NAME GIVEN TO THE EASTERN-MOST SPIT OF LAND FORMING PART OF THE PENINSULA OF CHALCIDICE. THE AREA IS STILL INHABITED BY 1,500 MONKS—WHERE ONCE THERE WERE MANY THOUSANDS—LIVING IN 20 MONASTERIES.

The Monasteries of Athos

FACT FILE

AD 963
Founding of Megisti Lavra, the first monastery.
972
Athos gains its first constitution. Its status as an independent monks' republic has been enshrined in law since 1912.
1453
Decline of Byzantium.
1988
Inscribed as a UNESCO World Heritage Site.

A ridge of mountains runs the entire length of the peninsula of Chalcidice, terminating in Mount Athos, a peak 6,670 ft/2,033 m high. The first community of monks, Megisti Lavra, was established here in AD 963, and most of the other monasteries that followed were founded between the tenth and fifteenth centuries. The community grew swiftly, and by 1100, there were already 45 monasteries on Athos. During its heyday, Athos was home to some 40,000 monks. The monks of this holy place—into which, under the strict Byzantine tradition, no women are permitted—have been responsible for administering their own justice. There is a state governor, but he deals only with general matters: Athos is an independent monks' republic. The governor represents the Greek state, which is in turn responsible for the independence of the republic. By making tribute payments to the Ottoman rulers, the monks even succeeded in retaining their autonomy during the period of Turkish rule between 1453 and 1912.

Above: The monastery-fortress of Stavronikita, dating from the sixteenth century, enjoys a commanding view over the Aegean Sea from its rocky spur on the north coast of Mount Athos.

The Monasteries of Metéora

NOT FAR FROM ATHOS, IN CENTRAL GREECE, ARE THE 24 MONASTERY-STRONGHOLDS OF METÉORA. PERCHED ON CLIFFTOPS, THESE MONASTERIES BEAR WITNESS TO AN UNBROKEN HISTORY OF GREEK ORTHODOX FAITH GOING BACK MANY CENTURIES.

The Monasteries of Metéora

The extraordinary sandstone cliffs at Metéora are 60 million years old. The first monasteries were built on these "heavenly pillars," as they were known to the ascetics, in the tenth century, as fortified structures capable of defending against enemy attack. By the end of the fifteenth century, there were 24 monasteries. These establishments experienced their heyday over the following period of nearly 200 years. Post-Byzantine paintings that have survived to the present day bear witness to this golden age. It is difficult to conceive the enormous effort involved in building these structures.

The monks reached their holy sanctuaries perched at dizzying heights either by climbing up ladders that were lashed together into long lengths or by being hauled up in nets in exactly the same way their supplies were. At one time, pilgrims used to be pulled up in nets to the monastery of Varlaám, which is located at a height of 1,230 ft/375 m. In 1920, steps were hewn into the rock and have made access a little easier. During World War II, many of the monasteries were bombarded and plundered. Today, only seven are active, inhabited by a small number of monks and nuns.

FACT FILE

Tenth century AD
First hermits' settlement established.
1370
Founding of the monastery Megálo Metéoro.
Since 1972
Regular conservation work carried out.
1988
Inscribed as a UNESCO World Heritage Site.

Above: The Metéora monastery of Varlaám. Metéora means something like "suspended in the air"— an entirely fitting description.

Left: The Metéora monastery of Agios Nikólaos Anapavsás, founded in the fourteenth century.

Rila Monastery

RILA MONASTERY, THE LARGEST MONASTIC COMPLEX IN BULGARIA AND ONE OF
THE MOST IMPRESSIVE SACRED SITES IN THE BALKANS, WAS FOUNDED OVER 1,000
YEARS AGO. IN ITS PRESENT FORM, IT STANDS AS A SYMBOL OF THE BULGARIAN
RENAISSANCE OF THE NINETEENTH CENTURY.

Tucked away in a high valley among forested slopes, at first glance the complex could be mistaken for a medieval fortress. It does indeed date from the Middle Ages, having been founded by the monk St. Ivan Rilski in the tenth century, but of the walls (or wooden structures) of the ancient monastery nothing remains. Only the oldest part of the monastery, the Tower of Hrelyu, which dominates the entire complex, is medieval; all the other parts date from the nineteenth century. In 1378, Rila Monastery was granted privileges by

Czar Ivan Shishman, ushering in a cultural golden age that left its mark on the monastic architecture and other arts practiced at the monastery.

This came to an end with the fall of Constantinople in 1453, which brought the heyday of Byzantine monastic architecture in general to a close and marked the beginning of a period of decline for most Orthodox monasteries, including Rila. During the sixteenth century, large numbers of monks emigrated to Russia. In 1833, the monastery was destroyed in a fire, but by this time, Bulgarian national consciousness had grown so strong that the main monastery church was rebuilt soon afterward, along with the distinctive galleried wing in the

FACT FILE

Tenth century AD
Founding of the monastery (originally a hermitage) by the monk St. Ivan Rilski.
1335–45
Construction of a defensive tower and church.
1833
Destruction of the monastery in a conflagration.
1834–50
Rebuilding of the monastery complex; church frescoes completed.
1961
Declared a national monument.
1983
Inscribed as a UNESCO World Heritage Site.

Left-hand page: View of the monastery complex with the Church of the Ascension. The monastery took on its current appearance at the time of its reconstruction in the nineteenth century.

Right: The arcading of the porch and main door to the Church of the Ascension. The austere coursed masonry contrasts strongly with the frescoed walls within.

monastery courtyard. The style of architecture was modeled on buildings in the monks' republic of Athos, in Greece, in particular the (Bulgarian) monastery of Zograf and the (Greek) monastery of Esphigmenou, both of which date from the beginning of the nineteenth century. The reconstruction of Rila Monastery thus symbolizes a return to a strong Orthodox and national identity. Around this time, Rila started to attract thousands of pilgrims each year, marking its reawakening as an important spiritual center. The church, a five-domed structure with two side chapels, impressed the faithful with its magnificent frescoes and a monumental iconostasis. The icons themselves, executed by some of Bulgaria's most important painters, restored to the church the air of sanctity it had once possessed.

Below left and right: Nineteenth-century frescoes in the porch of the church. Particularly impressive are the activities of the inhabitants of hell in the dramatic scenes of the Last Judgment.

Hagia Sophia

HAGIA SOPHIA (ΆΓΊΑ ΣΟΦΊΑ), THE CHURCH OF THE HOLY WISDOM, IN ISTANBUL, WAS ORIGINALLY A BYZANTINE CHURCH. IT WAS SUBSEQUENTLY TRANSFORMED INTO AN OTTOMAN MOSQUE AND, EVENTUALLY, A MUSEUM.

Of the Hagia Sophia built in the fourth century AD by Emperor Constantine, nothing remains. This was the most magnificent of a string of churches built by the first Christian Roman emperor in various cities throughout the empire. After it was destroyed, this first church was rebuilt by his son Constantius and Emperor Theodosius. During the Nika riots in 532, it burned down once more, along with half of the city. Nika was the name given to the chariot races held on the Hippodrome in front of the church, which involved frequent clashes between the supporters of the different teams. Between 532 and 537, Emperor Justinian I rebuilt the church as a showpiece of Byzantine architecture. It was richly decorated with mosaics and marble columns. After it was completed, he is said to have exclaimed, "O Solomon, I have outdone you."

For 900 years, Hagia Sophia was the seat of the Orthodox patriarch of Constantinople and the place where Church councils and imperial ceremonies were held. At the beginning of the thirteenth century, however, this sacred place was plundered and partially destroyed by Crusaders, and the patriarch was replaced by a Roman Catholic bishop. This exacerbated the

Hagia Sophia

FACT FILE

AD 532–37
Building of a new church under architects Isidore of Miletus and Anthemius of Tralles.

558
An earthquake causes the dome to collapse.

563
The dome collapses for a second time.

989 and 1346
Further damage to the dome caused by earthquakes.

1054
The Great Schism.

1204
Destruction and plundering of the church by Crusaders.

May 29, 1453
Sultan Mehmet transforms the church into a mosque.

1934
Secularization of the mosque by Kemal Atatürk.

1985
Inscribed as a UNESCO World Heritage Site.

Left-hand page: Hagia Sophia with the Bosphorus River and parts of the city in the background. The building's location is as impressive as its architecture.

Right: Interior of Hagia Sophia. This view has changed little since the years AD 532–37.

split between the Roman Catholic and Greek Orthodox churches that had begun with the Great Schism of 1054. Many of the treasures plundered from Hagia Sophia can be admired today in St. Mark's Basilica in Venice. Until 1453 and Sultan Mehmet's triumphal march into Constantinople, the church continued as a functioning place of worship. It was then turned into a mosque. At first, other than the addition of a wooden minaret and the construction of a prayer niche known as a mihrab, very little was changed. Over the course of time, however, all the mosaics featuring human portraits were covered over with plaster as Islam prohibits the depiction of the human figure. Over the following centuries, various sultans added buildings and transformed other parts of the church. Under the Turkish president Kemal Atatürk, the mosque was secularized and turned into the Ayasofya Museum.

Below: Interior mosaics: Mary and Child, flanked by Emperor John II Comnenus and Empress Irene, 1118.

Africa, known at one time as the "Dark Continent," is home to a diverse range of religions. These vary from the animistic beliefs of the continent's indigenous peoples to Islam and Judaism, and to various forms of Christianity, a number of whose sacred objects are to be found on Africa's soil. Not only is Africa the cradle of humanity, but—shrouded in the distant past—it also holds the secrets to the origins of human faith and religious practice.

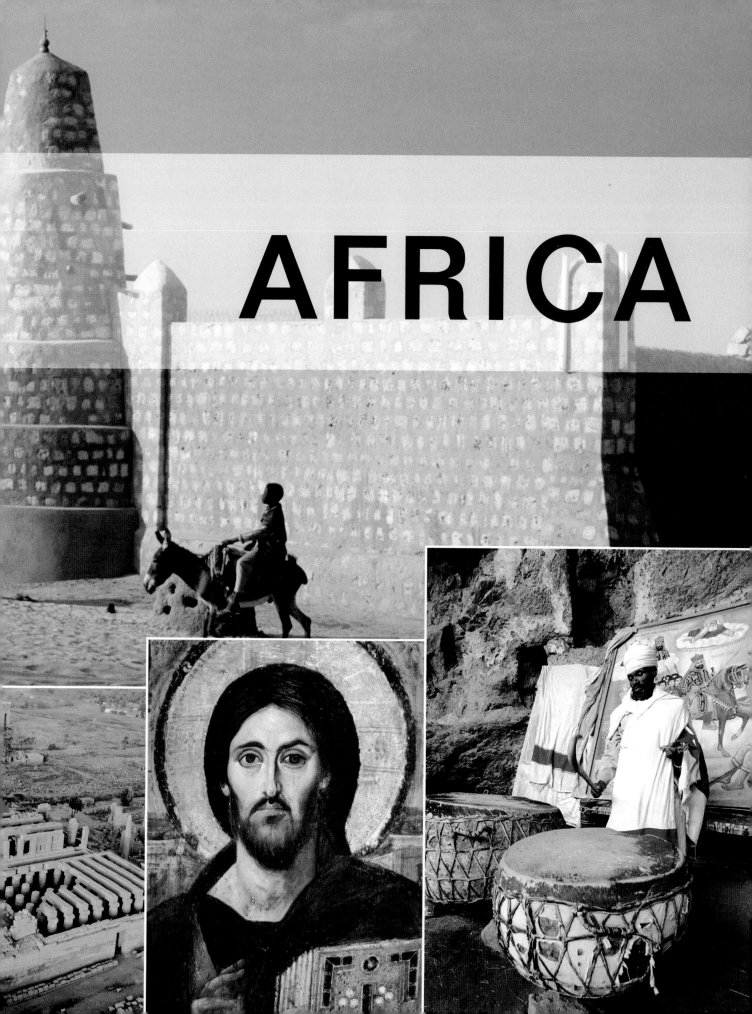

AFRICA

Kairouan

THE TUNISIAN CITY OF KAIROUAN IS ISLAM'S FOURTH MOST IMPORTANT HOLY SITE
AFTER MECCA, MEDINA, AND JERUSALEM. THE ARABS CONQUERED NORTH AFRICA
IN THE SEVENTH CENTURY AD, BRINGING WITH THEM THE HOLY WORD OF GOD.

When the Arabs entered Africa in the seventh century AD, their military commander, Uqba ibn Nafi (622–83), thrust his sword into the ground and founded Africa's first Arabic city and a center of learning and art. Kairouan, with its great mosque, became the Maghreb's principal holy city. This first mosque was taken as a model for all the mosques of North Africa, and even those of Spain. By the end of the seventh century—in other words, two or three generations after the emergence of Islam—the basic functions and typology of the great mosque had already been established. Kairouan means "army camp," and the city, indeed, has a militaristic past. It was threatened by Berbers, fought over by rival dynasties, and later became entangled in the religious wars between the Shiites and Sunnis. The walls of the holy city were razed and rebuilt no fewer than seven times. The Sidi Uqba Mosque, named after the founder of the city, was destroyed three times and rebuilt on each occasion. Its latest incarnation dates from the ninth century, when Kairouan was enjoying a golden age under the Aghlabids.

Kairouan's most important place of pilgrimage is the Zaouia Sidi Sahab (Barbier Mosque), dating from the

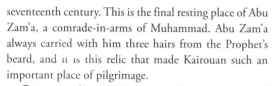

Left-hand page: Interior of the Sidi Uqba Mosque with its "forest of pillars." Every inch of the prayer hall floor is covered with carpets.

Right: Muslim pilgrim in front of a tiled wall in the Barbier Mosque.

seventeenth century. This is the final resting place of Abu Zam'a, a comrade-in-arms of Muhammad. Abu Zam'a always carried with him three hairs from the Prophet's beard, and it is this relic that made Kairouan such an important place of pilgrimage.

Return to the city. Kairouan's old town is a mass of winding lanes where time seems to stand still. It is divided into districts by trade and clan, or family affiliations, and contains more than 120 mausolea and mosques of all sizes and featuring every style of decoration. For the Muslim faithful, three trips to Kairouan are the equivalent of one pilgrimage to Mecca. Behind the blue entrance to the seventeenth-century Bir Barouta Well—once the city's main water distribution point—visitors are greeted by the sight of a camel working a water wheel. There is a legend that Bir Barouta is connected below ground with Mecca's holy spring of Zamzam. It is said that whoever drinks of this water will return to the holy city in the Saudi Arabian desert.

FACT FILE

AD 670
Founding of the city (according to legend).
672
Work on the Sidi Uqba Mosque started.
1618
Fifth enlargement and remodeling of the Sidi Uqba Mosque.
1988
Inscribed as a UNESCO World Heritage Site.

Right: One of Kairouan's many multiple-domed mosques.

EGYPT

Abu Mena

ACCORDING TO LEGEND, ST. MENAS WAS A ROMAN LEGIONARY WHO WITHDREW TO THE DESERT AS A CHRISTIAN HERMIT AND EVENTUALLY DIED A MARTYR'S DEATH. HIS FUNERARY CHURCH AND BAPTISTERY WERE TO BECOME EGYPT'S MOST IMPORTANT PLACE OF CHRISTIAN PILGRIMAGE.

St. Menas is venerated as the patron saint of merchants and is also invoked for help in finding lost things. After a period of service in the Roman army, he chose an eremitic vocation. Subsequently, during the persecution of the Christians under Emperor Diocletian (AD 243–313), St. Menas was tortured, beheaded, and buried in the Egyptian desert near Alexandria. In 380, Emperor Theodosius (349–95) officially adopted Christianity as the state religion of the Roman Empire. Thousands of pilgrims came to Abu Mena to be accepted into the new faith. The town grew

prosperous and developed into North Africa's largest center of pilgrimage. Due to the crowds of pilgrims it attracted, the town has been nicknamed the "Lourdes of ancient Christendom." Many miracles are reported to have occurred there, and it is even said that the dead have been brought back to life. Each day, thousands of believers gathered on the pilgrims' square, and the numerous inns of what was then a magnificent town were filled with the lame, the blind, and lepers. Until the eleventh century, pilgrims came to Abu Mena from all over the Christian world and took healing oil back home with them. With the rise and eventual dominance of Islam, however, the town gradually fell into decline.

Abu Mena

FACT FILE

AD 296
Martyrdom of St. Menas.
Fifth/sixth centuries
Construction of
the baptistery.
Seventh/eighth centuries
Construction of a triple-
aisled basilica.
Circa 1300
Abu Mena abandoned.
1905
Excavations by Carl
Maria Kaufmann.
1979
Inscribed as a UNESCO
World Heritage Site.

Below left and right: In
addition to modest stone
and brick ruins, exquisitely
sculpted capitals have also
been discovered. Egypt's
Christians, the Copts, who
revived Abu Mena as a
place of pilgrimage in the
twentieth century, are once
again facing the prospect of
losing their holy site.

Left-hand page and right:
Ancient ruins at Abu Mena.
The heart of the complex
was a 400-ft/120-m
enfilade of liturgical rooms
consisting of an octagonal
baptistery, a quadruple-
apsed chapel adjoining to
the east—constructed over
the martyr's tomb during the
time of Justinian (reigned
AD 527–65)—and the great
cruciform basilica, dating
from around AD 500.

Under threat. The town was plundered, burned
down, and covered by sand before being rediscovered
nearly 1,000 years later by an archaeologist from
Frankfurt. The city in the desert has once again
regained its status as the Copts' (Egyptian Christians)
most important place of pilgrimage, and Coptic monks
have established a new monastery here. However,
Abu Mena is now under threat once more. The Nile
River is being canalized, and what was once desert is
being crisscrossed by numerous canals in a job-creation
scheme centering on the Nile. For Abu Mena, this
could mean disaster. Its walls are being destroyed by
rising ground water; many of the underground structures
have already been submerged; and in several places,
there is the danger of imminent collapse. Abu Mena is
on UNESCO's World Heritage red-alert list, but it can
only be saved by putting an end to canalization.

The Great Pyramids of Giza

THE GREAT PYRAMIDS OF GIZA ARE THE BEST-KNOWN OF ALL PYRAMIDS AND THE LAST SURVIVING WONDER OF THE ANCIENT WORLD. AS THE TOMBS OF EGYPT'S "GOD-KINGS," THEY WERE REVERED MORE THAN 4,000 YEARS AGO AS PLACES OF GREAT HOLINESS.

The Great
Pyramids of Giza

There are nine pyramids at Giza, plus the famous Great Sphinx (a figure of a recumbent lion with a human head). Originally, this mythical creature symbolized the "divine" kingdom of the pharaohs of the Fourth Dynasty (2639–2504 BC), but at a later stage, it came to be associated with the sun god Horus.

The pharaohs who built the most magnificent pyramids as their tombs were Cheops, Chephren, and Mycerinus, around 2585–2520 BC. It took 30,000 workers more than 30 years, using in excess of 2.3 million stone blocks, to build the enormous Pyramid of Cheops, which still stands in the desert today as a symbol of a past godhead. The passages in the interior of the pyramid are sealed with large stone blocks. But they could not prevent grave robbers, even in ancient times, from gaining access. As a result, pyramid tombs were often plundered. Many pyramids were found to contain nothing but an empty granite sarcophagus. Southwest of the Pyramid of Cheops is Chephren's tomb, and southwest of that is the smallest of the three pyramids—that of Mycerinus. The external walls of the pyramids were originally surfaced with panels of limestone, of which only fragments now remain.

FACT FILE

Great Sphinx
Built: around 2590 BC.
Height: 241 ft/73.5 m
Length: 66 ft/20 m
Width: 20 ft/6 m

Pyramid of Cheops
Built: around 2585 BC.
Height: 453 ft/138 m,
originally 481 ft/146.5 m
Length of sides: 756 ft/
230.33 m
Volume: 91,227,778 cu ft/
2,583,283 cu m
Angle of slope: 51° 50'

Pyramid of Chephren
Built: around 2550 BC.
Height: 469 ft/143 m,
originally 471 ft/143.5 m
Length of sides: 705 ft/215 m
Volume: 78,084,118 cu ft/
2,211,096 cu m
Angle of slope: 53° 10'

Pyramid of Mycerinus
Built: around 2520 BC.
Height: 203 ft/62 m,
originally 215 ft/65.55 m
Length of sides: 335 ft/102 m
Volume: 8,516,308 cu ft/
241,155 cu m
Angle of slope: 51° 20'

Left-hand page: The group of three main pyramids at Giza: those of Cheops, Chephren, and Mycerinus. The pyramids were once surfaced with white limestone, which was removed centuries ago.

Right: The Great Gallery in the Pyramid of Cheops, involving the successful covering of a wide corridor with powerful forces weighing down on it, is regarded as a wonder of structural engineering.

The cult of the dead. The oldest pyramids date from the period circa 2680–2600 BC. They include the Step Pyramid in the tomb precinct of King Djoser at Saqqara (the oldest monumental building in the world, dating from around 2680 BC) and the so-called "Bent Pyramid" and Red Pyramid, both of which were built at Meidum by Pharaoh Snefru. These early pyramids are regarded as models for all the Egyptian pyramids that followed.

The pyramids are aligned with the points of the compass. On the north sides are the entrances to the tombs; to the east are the cult chapels for the deceased. Originally, burial chambers were sunk into the ground, whereas later they were concealed within the masonry.

Below: The Great Sphinx, a mythical creature with the head of a man and the body of a lion, can be seen as a monumental image of the ruler, impressively symbolizing the "divine" kingdom of the pharaohs during the earlier years of the Fourth Dynasty (2639–2504 BC). Later, during the New Kingdom (1550–1070 BC), the Great Sphinx came to embody the sun god Horus.

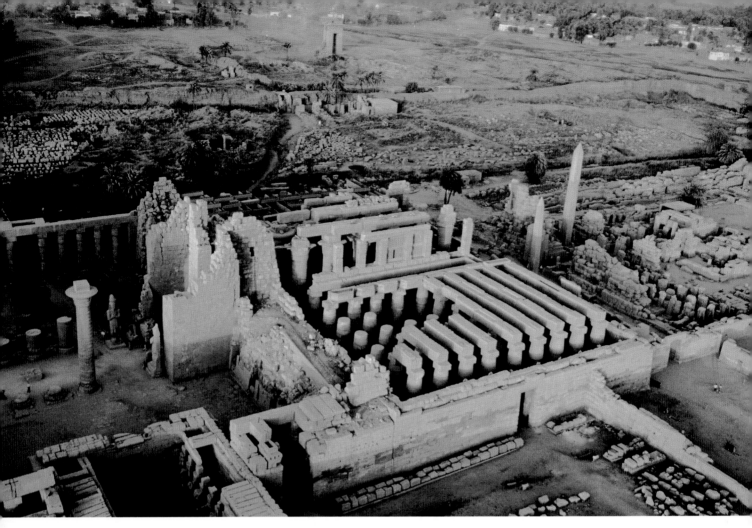

EGYPT

EGYPT

Karnak

Karnak

THE TEMPLE COMPLEX AT KARNAK, DEDICATED TO THE GOD AMUN-RE, GREW INTO AN ENORMOUS TEMPLE CITY DURING THE COURSE OF THE NEW KINGDOM. IN ITS DAY, IT WAS THE LARGEST COMPLEX OF SACRED BUILDINGS IN THE WORLD AND EGYPT'S MOST IMPORTANT SHRINE.

FACT FILE

2019–1794 BC
Middle Kingdom.
1956–1911 BC
Construction begun by
Sesostris I during the
Twelfth Dynasty.
1550–1070 BC
New Kingdom.
Circa 1450 BC
Major building phase under
Thutmosis II during the
Eighteenth Dynasty.
1979
Inscribed as a UNESCO
World Heritage Site.

Amun-Re, whose name means "master of the invisible breath of light that animates all things," was originally the local deity of the city of Thebes, but he came to be regarded as the god of all other gods who coexisted with him. The monumental temple at Karnak can be seen as an embodiment in stone of his cult. The complex was extended by pharaoh after pharaoh and dynasty after dynasty. Along with its various dependencies and estates, the temple had 70,000 priests, headed by a high priest and three "divine servers" who supported the king in his role as supreme cult head. The roof of this temple, adorned with magnificent wall and ceiling paintings, was once supported by 134 columns decorated with reliefs and hieroglyphs. The main shrine was located behind the rows of columns in the inner chamber. The complex also included the temples of Mut to the north and Khonsu to the south. The site was linked to the city of Luxor about 1½ miles/2.5 km away by a splendid processional road, and another broad ceremonial avenue led to a mooring point on the Nile. The combination of different architectural styles at the enormous complex indicates that each ruler made additions to the main structure over the course of the centuries.

Above: Aerial view of the ruins of the extensive temple complex at Karnak.

Luxor

THE TEMPLE COMPLEX AT LUXOR WAS REGARDED AS THE MAIN SHRINE AND
SOUTHERN RESIDENCE OF THE DEITY AMUN-RE. IT SERVED THE GOD AS A PLACE
OF COSMIC RENEWAL AND REGENERATION, AND PROVIDED A SETTING FOR THE
RECONFIRMING OF THE KING'S DIVINE STATUS.

Luxor

The construction of the temple complex at Luxor was begun under the Thutmosid rulers of the Eighteenth Dynasty. Their main temple was replaced around 1380 BC, during the reign of Amenophis III, by a monumental new structure that was subsequently added to, notably by Tutankhamun and Ramses II. In addition to splendid reliefs, the complex also possesses monumental statues of Ramses II. The temple in Luxor (ancient Thebes) was designed as a venue for major ceremonies in honor of Amun-Re. It was linked to the shrine at Karnak by a processional avenue which was lined with hundreds of sphinxes and stretched

for 2 miles/3.2 km. During the Feast of Opet—Ancient Egypt's largest festival, dedicated to the rising water level of the Nile River—statues of Amun-Re and other gods were transported by barge with great pomp from Karnak to Luxor. Their arrival at the Temple of Luxor was greeted by dancers and musicians, and over a period of several days, amid great ceremony, rituals aimed at consolidating the power of the "god-king" were performed. The annual deification of the living king and his power took place in the audience room behind the great columned hall. Everything at Luxor was magnificent and conceived on a large scale.

FACT FILE

**Main temple built by and
added to by the following:**
Amenophis III
1402–1364 BC.
Amenophis IV
1364–1347 BC.
Tutankhamun
Circa 1347–1339 BC.
Ramses II
Circa 1298–1213 BC.

1836
One of the obelisks of the
Temple of Luxor is
transported to Paris, where
it still stands in the Place de
la Concorde.
1995
Discovery of the
mausoleum of the sons
of Ramses II.
1979
Inscribed as a UNESCO
World Heritage Site.

Above: One of the
numerous royal reliefs at
the Temple of Luxor.

Left: A colossal seated figure
of Ramses II at the Temple of
Luxor—circa 1220 BC, height
approximately 23 ft/7 m.
This statue of the enthroned
figure bears its own name:
Ra-en-hekau, meaning "sun
of the foreign rulers."

SINAI/EGYPT

St. Catherine's Monastery

ST. CATHERINE'S MONASTERY, ONE OF THE MOST FAMOUS OF ALL THE MIDDLE
EASTERN DESERT MONASTERIES, IS LOCATED BELOW MOUNT SINAI ON THE SINAI
PENINSULA. IT PERPETUATES THE MEMORY OF THE BURNING BUSH AND POSSESSES
A COLLECTION OF WONDERFUL EARLY BYZANTINE ICONS THAT WERE MADE HERE.

St. Catherine's
Monastery

The monastery was founded between AD 548
and 565. According to inscriptions found
on the roof beams, the church and parts of
the tower positioned in front of it also date from the
sixth century. These inscriptions name
Emperor Justinian, Empress Theodora,
and an architect from Aqaba. Until
the nineteenth century, the monastic
buildings were continually replaced and
renewed. The general appearance of
the monastery is dominated by its high
perimeter wall, erected in the seventh
century to afford protection against

bands of wandering thieves and Arab raiders. Thanks
to its isolated location, St. Catherine's is one of the few
monasteries never to have been destroyed.

The unique holiness of this place. The location
of the monastery is a reminder that Moses received the
Ten Commandments from God on Mount Sinai (Exodus
19–20). Furthermore, the burning bush in which God
revealed himself to Moses (Exodus 3:2) is venerated
in a chapel behind the apse of the monastery church,
increasing the sanctity of the place still more. The relics
of St. Catherine of Alexandria, a martyr from the third
or fourth century from whom the monastery takes its
name, were acquired at a later date.

FACT FILE

Fourth century AD
Monks settle in the area and build a chapel dedicated to the Virgin Mary.
548–65
Founding and construction of the existing monastic complex.
Circa 610
St. John Climacus writes *The Ladder to Paradise*.
Eighth–ninth centuries
Byzantine Iconoclasm, which the monastery's icons survive unscathed.
1844
Discovery by Konstantin von Tischendorf of the Codex Sinaiticus, the oldest near-complete manuscript of the Bible.
2002
Inscribed as a UNESCO World Heritage Site.

Left-hand page: A high wall was built around the sixth-century St. Catherine's Monastery to protect it against marauders.

Right: This icon of Christ, dating from the sixth/seventh centuries AD, presents the face of a middle-aged man whose "authenticity" is achieved by subtle artistic means.

Monastic treasures. The monastery library, considered the oldest surviving Christian library in the world, is priceless. Among the many manuscripts in its keeping is the famous treatise *The Ladder to Paradise*, one of the most influential works of Orthodox spirituality. Its author, St. John Climacus, is thought to have been one of the hermits who lived in the vicinity of the monastery, seeking protection behind its walls only during times of danger.

The monastery's treasures also include over 2,000 icons. Some of them date from the Early Byzantine period and survived the Byzantine Iconoclasm of the eighth and ninth centuries unscathed, making them extremely rare. Among the most famous of the ancient icons from the sixth and seventh centuries is the one of Christ illustrated here.

Left and above: The richly appointed and decorated church interior includes precious mosaics from the Justinian era.

Timbuktu

TIMBUKTU IS AN ALMOST MYTHICAL CITY IN THE MALIAN DESERT. DOMINATED BY
SAND, IT POSSESSES THREE GREAT MOSQUES FROM THE FOURTEENTH, FIFTEENTH,
AND SIXTEENTH CENTURIES, AS WELL AS CEMETERIES AND MAUSOLEA MADE OF
BROWN EARTH.

Viewed from a distance, Timbuktu looks like a collection of brown mud cubes cowering from the omnipresent sand. Three mosques stand out clearly from the cubes with their elongated, rounded forms. When Timbuktu fell under the influence of the Mali Empire in the thirteenth century, it was immediately converted to Islam, but it was more than 100 years before the city became a place of pilgrimage. The first two mosques, the Djingareyber and the Sankoré, were constructed of earth in the fourteenth and fifteenth centuries, respectively. The

fact that they are made of earth, however, provides for laborious upkeep because the mud plaster has to be repaired after each rainy season. The minarets of the mosques are constructed around a skeleton of wooden poles in order to hold the soft building material in place. During the fifteenth century, the Sankoré Mosque was developed into a university comprising a number of different Qur'an schools. Venerated as a holy place, students came from all over the Islamic world to study and pray in the mosque's inner courtyard. Sidi Yahia, dating from the sixteenth century, is the least venerable of the three mosques. Unlike the other two, this one is made of stone. Today, it houses a modern Qur'an school for the city's children. Timbuktu

Timbuktu

FACT FILE

Number of inhabitants today
Approximately 35,000.
Circa AD 1000
First mentioned in Arabic chronicles.
1327
Construction of Djingareyber Mosque.
Fourteenth–sixteenth centuries
Develops into a religious and economic center.
1828
Frenchman René Caillé spends 11 days in Timbuktu.
1894
The French conquer the city.
1988
Inscribed as a UNESCO World Heritage Site.

Left-hand page: Sankoré Mosque, built in the fifteenth century, was also used as a university or institute of higher education.

Below: View across Timbuktu's earth-colored buildings. Many of the clay houses have an ingenious air-conditioning system.

Left: The market square is one of the focuses of the city's social life, which, in the Islam world, takes place increasingly under the supervision of religion, even in Africa.

experienced its cultural and spiritual golden age in the fifteenth and sixteenth centuries, when it is thought to have had up to 180 Qur'an schools.

Closed to non-Muslims. For Europeans, Timbuktu has always been more of a mirage than a real place. Not only was it fragile and apparently built of sand, but also food had to be brought in from hundreds of miles away along the Niger River. In the nineteenth century, non-Muslims were prohibited from entering Timbuktu, although in 1826, Alexander Gordon Laing, a British officer, became the first European to reach the city. He lived there for a time, but was killed by a religious fanatic while returning to Morocco. Another European to make it to Timbuktu—with the help of Arabic-speaking Tuareg guides—was the German Africa explorer Heinrich Barth. He spoke perfect Arabic and spent the years 1853–54 in the city studying the lives of its inhabitants under the assumed name Abd El Kerim. Once he was discovered, he was forced to flee. Today, the city can be freely visited, but little remains of its former splendor. With a few exceptions, the historical city center became impoverished and was turned into a wasteland as a result of the civil war with the Tuareg (1990–96).

Aksum

IN THE HOLY CITY OF AKSUM IS ETHIOPIA'S MOST SACRED SITE—THE CHURCH OF ST. MARY OF ZION, WHICH DATES FROM THE SEVENTEENTH CENTURY. A RELIQUARY CHAPEL NEXT DOOR TO IT IS SAID TO CONTAIN THE FAMOUS ARK OF THE COVENANT.

Aksum lies on the ancient caravan routes to Arabia, Nubia, and Egypt, and once enjoyed a vigorous trade with the Red Sea and Indian Ocean ports, as well as with Rome, Greece, and Constantinople. The oldest Christian realm in the world—and the largest outside the Roman Empire—emerged here, with Aksum as the holiest city in the Ethiopian Orthodox faith. Although the present church is relatively recent, its foundations are impressively ancient. In his youth, St. Ezana, king of Ethiopia in the fourth century, was converted to Christianity by two Syrian monks and introduced Christianity into the kingdom once he came to the throne. Just before his death, Ezana made Frumentius, one of his two Syrian teachers, head of the Ethiopian Church. St. Frumentius built a church dedicated to the Holy Virgin, which stood for hundreds of years before being destroyed by Muslims in the sixteenth century. At the beginning of the seventeenth century, Emperor Fasilides (1632–67) raised a new church, the one that still stands today, over the ruins of its predecessor. Not only is the Church of St. Mary of Zion a symbol of the strength of the Ethiopian Orthodox faith, but it also stands for the strength of the Ethiopian nation itself. The church has been used for the coronations of

Aksum

Left-hand page: The Church of St. Mary of Zion, probably built in the fourth century AD, is the oldest and most important Ethiopian Orthodox church.

Right: Wall paintings in the church. The depictions of the saints, thought to date from the seventeenth century, are heavily stylized and extremely colorful.

all Ethiopian emperors and, until the 1930s, provided criminals with amnesty from the law. Haile Selassie, the last leader of the Solomonic dynasty, built a new Church of St. Mary of Zion next to the old one, as well as a reliquary chapel designed to provide the Ark of the Covenant, which has supposedly been held here since the time of King Solomon, with a worthy home.

Rift with the universal church. In the late fifth century, the Christian faith was disseminated among the general population by missionaries who had fled from the Eastern Roman Empire. These missionaries were Monophysites—that is, they adhered to the ancient Christian belief that Christ had one inseparable nature rather than two (a divine one and a human one). The Monophysite doctrine was prohibited at the Council of Chalcedon, held in Bithynia, Asia Minor, in 451, in favor of the two-nature doctrine, and the proponents of the Monophysite doctrine were condemned as heretics and blasphemers. This divergence in belief caused the Coptic, Ethiopian, Armenian, and Syrian-Jacobite Churches to break away from the universal Church. The Monophysite doctrine remains an integral part of Ethiopian Orthodox belief to this day.

FACT FILE

Fourth century AD
Construction of the first Church of St. Mary of Zion.
Mid-sixteenth century
Destruction of the church by the troops of Ahmed Gragn.
1635
Rebuilding of the church by Emperor Fasilides.
1955–64
Construction of a new church by Emperor Haile Selassie.
1980
Inscribed as a UNESCO World Heritage Site.

Left: A deacon holding a sistrum (an ancient North African hand rattle) in front of the reliquary chapel. The Ethiopian Ark of the Covenant may only be looked upon when uncovered by its attendant.

ETHIOPIA

Lalibela

OVER 800 YEARS AGO, UNKNOWN STONEMASONS BUILT A GROUP OF CHURCHES, MANY OF THEM SEVERAL STORIES HIGH, IN RED VOLCANIC ROCK. THEY ARE KNOWN AS THE HOLY ROCK-HEWN CHURCHES OF LALIBELA, LOCATED IN ETHIOPIA IN THE HORN OF AFRICA.

Lalibela, located in the mountains of Ethiopia at a height of 8,530 ft/2,600 m, is still visited today by devout Orthodox pilgrims who venerate the place as a second Jerusalem. The rock-cut churches have been executed with consummate mastery, giving rise to a legend that angels assisted with their construction, because men would never have been able to create such marvels unaided. Between the twelfth and thirteenth centuries, a total of 11 churches were carved out of the red basalt, most with more than one story. A distinction is made between so-called monoliths (those that have been hewn from a single block), semimonoliths (those whose facade alone is of one piece), and the cave churches built into a natural cavern. The northern cluster of buildings includes Bet Medhane Alem, the largest monolithic church in the world, and Bet Maryam, the oldest (*Bet* means "house"). Bet Golgotha (meaning "the house of Golgotha") houses the tomb of the holy emperor Lalibela. The church now known as Bet Gabriel-Rufael was once the royal palace.

The holy sanctuaries of a labyrinthine city. Legend has it that when Jerusalem was conquered by the Arabs under Saladin in 1187, the saintly emperor Gebra

Lalibela ●

FACT FILE

Fifth century AD
Dissemination of the Christian faith throughout Ethiopia.
Ninth century
Advance of Islam and the decline of the Aksum Empire.
Twelfth/thirteenth centuries
Under Emperor Lalibela, golden age of the Zagwe dynasty in Ethiopia; construction of 11 monolithic rock-hewn churches within a time period of approximately 120 years to create a "New Jerusalem."
1978
Inscribed as a UNESCO World Heritage Site.

Left-hand page: Bet Abba Libanos, which is built into the cliffside. It is more a sculptural than an architectonic achievement.

Right: Orthodox priest drumming in one of the rock churches. Behind him is a religious canvas serving a didactic purpose.

Maskal Lalibela ordained that it should be reconstructed in the Horn of Africa "out of a single stone." It is still not known how the gifted thirteenth-century craftspeople responsible for the churches achieved their feat, for the art of working stone in this way and the knowledge of which stone is best suited to being carved into a monolithic edifice using nothing but chisels have been lost over the centuries. What is most impressive about the skill of these medieval stonemasons is that they carved all the interior furnishings, wall moldings, and decorations by hand out of the same block of stone. Cornices, windows, and steps were therefore carved into the rock before it was hollowed out and pillars, arches, and niches created inside. The churches are connected via passageways and staircases in order to allow easy movement between the many holy sites of this mysterious labyrinthine Ethiopian Orthodox city.

Below left and right: Aerial and side view of Bet Giyorgis (Church of St. George), one of the most impressive of Lalibela's 11 churches.

Tsodilo Hills

THE SAN BUSHMEN, WHOSE FAMILY TREE REACHES BACK TO THE EARLIEST DAYS OF
HUMAN HISTORY, WERE THE FIRST INHABITANTS OF SOUTHERN AFRICA. SACRED TO
THEM TO THIS DAY ARE THE TSODILO HILLS, WITH THEIR COUNTLESS CAVES AND
ROCK DRAWINGS.

Rising to 4,885 ft/1,489 m, the Tsodilo Hills in the Kalahari Desert are the highest elevation for hundreds of miles around and Botswana's highest point. The four main peaks of these hills in the vicinity of the Okavango River delta are famous for their rock art (4,500 or so examples), which has earned them the nickname "Louvre of the Desert." An area measuring approximately 4 square miles/10 sq km contains the largest number of rock paintings in the world. These images tell of human existence during prehistoric times and of the changes in the environment that have occurred over a period of 100,000 years. The San people revere the Tsodilo Hills as the abode of their ancestors' spirits. The "realm of the ancestors" is an important concept in Africa. The San are adherents of an animistic religion: They consult an oracle of pottery fragments, fear spirits they believe have the power to make them ill, and seek healing through transcendental dancing. Their shamans are generally old women with spiritual powers. In the San's creation myth, the largest of the four rocky outcrops is the "man," the next largest is the "woman," and the second smallest is the "child." The smallest is the man's first wife, whom he abandoned for a younger woman.

Tsodilo
Hills

FACT FILE

Tsodilo
The largest collection of rock drawings in the world (approximately 4,500); evidence of human activity going back some 100,000 years.
2001
Inscribed as a UNESCO World Heritage Site.

The San people
The San arrived in southern Africa, where they lived as nomadic hunter-gatherers, around 25,000 years ago. The San are small of build but are not pygmies. Their stature ranges from 4 ft 7 inches/1.4 m to 5 ft 3 inches/1.6 m. There are now only 50,000 or so San living in Botswana.

Left-hand page, right, and below: Rock faces decorated with paintings, mostly of animals. This is typical of nomadic hunter-gatherer culture.

In 2001, a museum was opened at the site in order to provide information about the history of the area and the significance of the rock drawings.

A place of ancient ritual. In one of the caves, archaeologists found a stone approximately 7 ft/2 m long carved like a python and decorated with scales. Further investigations have revealed more than 13,000 artifacts and cave art created some 70,000 years ago. Among the finds are red spearheads that have been ceremonially burned. Behind the python stone was a small chamber used by shamans for rituals. The archaeological finds reveal that the inhabitants of this region had been holding rituals here 30,000 years earlier than was assumed.

Not only is Asia the biggest and most populous continent on earth, it is also the continent on which the largest number of religions is practiced. Asia is home to the most sacred sites of Buddhism, Hinduism, Shinto, Islam, and countless animistic religions. No other continent accommodates as many members of as many different faith communities—nor has as many regions whose religious harmony is currently under threat.

ASIA

Sacred Mount Fuji

MOUNT FUJI, KNOWN TO THE JAPANESE AS FUJI-SAN, IS THE MOST CLIMBED AND MOST HIGHLY MARKETED MOUNTAIN IN THE WORLD. ITS IMAGE HAS BECOME VIRTUALLY SYNONYMOUS WITH JAPAN. AS THE SEAT OF JAPAN'S SHINTO DEITIES, HOWEVER, IT IS ALSO THE COUNTRY'S MOST SACRED MOUNTAIN.

Japan's highest mountain, which has the perfect stratovolcano shape, is located some 60 miles/100 km west of Tokyo on the main island of Honshu. On clear winter days, Mount Fuji can easily be seen from the metropolis. The geological history of this sacred mountain began some 100,000 years ago. It stands on the point where the Eurasian, North American, and Filipino tectonic plates meet. The volcano's last eruption, in 1707, was so violent that even Edo (as Tokyo was then known) was covered by a layer of ash 6 inches/15 cm thick.

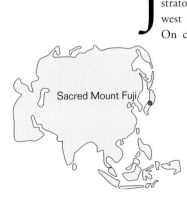

Sacred Mount Fuji

Shinto's most sacred mountain. In winter, Fuji, like every other mountain in Japan, is the abode of the mountain gods. The faithful are prohibited from climbing it at this time of year. The volcano is Shinto's most sacred mountain. Central to the Shinto religion is the belief in *kami* ("higher beings" or "deities"). These deities are not to be understood as preexisting or almighty but simply as "spiritual forces that are recognized as playing a part in the creation of all the things in the universe." The mountain, at which the deity is present, is the focal point of religious life. During the "snow free" time of year, when the mountain gods have left their mountaintops for the rice fields of the plains, Mount Fuji is opened to

FACT FILE

The "new" Fuji acquired its current shape about 10,000 years ago. Its climbing season has been fixed as July 1 to August 31.

Height:
12,388 ft/3,776 m

First ascent
By an unknown monk in
AD 663

Visitors
Approximately two million, of whom 200,000 make it to the summit.

Last eruption
December 16, 1707 (lasting around two weeks).

Right: This photograph shows a pilgrim on his way to the summit of Mount Fuji on Honshu Island around 1880.

climbers. On the first day of the sixth lunar month, the Yamabiraki ceremony is held to mark the official opening of the mountain. This ceremony involves a priest cutting a rope suspended between the posts of a *torii* (traditional Shinto gateway). Most pilgrims climb Mount Fuji at night because the best chance of being able to enjoy the view is early in the morning (the mountain is often shrouded in thick clouds during the summer). They generally take the cable car up to one of the intermediate stations and begin their ascent from a height of between 4,600 ft/1,400 m and 7,900 ft/2,400 m. The path up the sacred mountain is closed again on the twenty-seventh day of the seventh lunar month.

Left-hand page: Mount Fuji is a composite volcano (or stratovolcano), indicated by its conical shape.

Below left: Pilgrims press coins into posts at a Shinto shrine on Mount Fuji as gifts to the kami.

Below right: A typical wayside altar with offerings of mandarins, an apple, incense, and flowers.

Shinto Shrine on Itsukushima

THE ISLAND OF ITSUKUSHIMA HAS BEEN SACRED TO SHINTOISM SINCE TIME IMMEMORIAL. IT WAS ONCE FORBIDDEN TO SET FOOT UPON THE ISLAND, WHICH IS WHY THE SHRINE ITSELF WAS BUILT ON STILTS IN THE WATER.

According to Shinto legend, the god Izanagi and goddess Izanami thrust their jeweled spear into the ocean and the droplets that fell from it as they withdrew it from the water formed the islands that make up Japan. In the Shinto religion, natural forces, mountains, lakes, animals, trees, and—above all—ancestors are regarded as *kami* (or deities). Influenced by Confucianism, Taoism, and Buddhism, Shinto has neither founders nor holy texts, doctrines or precepts. It is dominated by a belief in the immortality of the soul. The Shinto faithful are expected to live at one with nature and to promote the harmony of their community. Everything that goes against this is regarded as debased. The essence of the religion—veneration of nature and one's ancestors—has remained unchanged from the earliest times.

Oneness with nature. In AD 593, when the first shrine was constructed on Itsukushima, those responsible did not dare build it directly on the ground because the island was (and still is) sacred. It was erected instead on posts in the mud of the shoreline because mortals were not allowed to set foot on the island. It is for this reason that the monumental red *torii* gateway, now an emblem of Japan, stands in the waters of the bay in front

Shinto Shrine on Itsukushima

FACT FILE

AD **593**
Construction of the first
shrine under Empress Suiko.
881
First documented mention
of shrine.
1164
Construction of the
main shrine.
1207 and 1223
Shrine destroyed by fire.
1571
Construction of the
current shrine.
1996
Inscribed as a UNESCO
World Heritage Site.

Above: In Shinto, an emphasis is placed on cleanliness. There are abundant fountains and water basins where visitors can wash and rinse their mouths.

Above: Shinto has millions of gods. The focus of religious life is therefore on the shrine rather than a specific god.

Left-hand page: At high tide, the torii (or entrance) to the shrine stands in the sea. It can only be reached when the water recedes. For this reason, it is called the "floating" or "drifting" torii.

of the shrine. At low tide, the shrine can be reached by foot; when the tide is in, it stands in the sea. The almost delicate wooden complex, with its hundreds of red pillars, wide open rooms, and transparent design, symbolizes the freedom of the kami to come and go as they please. What makes the Itsukushima shrine so special is its outstanding inherent beauty, for magnificent altars, statues, and images of deities are alien to Shinto. The entire island is "god," and so there is no need to portray anything. The shrine is open-walled.

Its interior is at one with the nature that surrounds it. There are numerous water basins where the faithful pause to wash and rinse their mouths—the only rule in Shinto is inner and outer purity.

Below: Hundreds of red pillars edge the temple.

Todai-ji

THE NAME OF THIS SACRED BUDDHIST SITE IN NARA AT THE SOUTHERN TIP OF HONSHU ISLAND MEANS "LARGE TEMPLE IN THE EAST." IN THE EIGHTH CENTURY AD, NARA WAS THE CAPITAL OF JAPAN.

Todai-ji was built as Japan's most important Buddhist temple by Emperor Shomu in AD 752, during the heyday of the Nara era. As well as being a monastery and a place of prayer, it controlled a network of Buddhist monasteries that extended throughout Japan. Its colossal dimensions are typical of the imperial architecture of the day. The temple and monastery grew so powerful that in 784, the capital was moved from Nara to Nagaoka in order to lessen their influence on the government. The sacred site was repeatedly destroyed by fire and

earthquake, and then rebuilt. In 1180, under Abbot Shunjobo Chogen (1121–1206), Todai-ji was rebuilt in the Chinese style following an earthquake. These stylistic influences can be seen today at the southern portal (Nandaimon), for which, in 1203, the sculptors Unkei and Kaikei created statues of two guardian gods some 26 ft/8 m tall. The current temple dates from 1709 and covers just two-thirds of its original surface area.

The Buddha opens his eyes. Today, the temple is the seat of the Buddhist Kegon sect, whose followers revere Buddha Vairocana (meaning "sun-like"), the ruler whose essence flows through the cosmos. The interior of the temple is dominated by an immense bronze

FACT FILE

AD 710–784
Nara era.
724–49
Reign of Emperor Shomu.
752–98
Construction of Todai-ji.

The monumental statue of the Buddha is made of copper and bronze, and its hair is made up of 988 bronze spheres.
Weight: 276 tons/ 250 tonnes
Height: 98 ft/30 m with plinth

Left-hand page: Todai-ji, which dates from the year 752, is the largest wooden building in the world.

Right: Buddhist monks and volunteers clean the statue of the Buddha, which is 52 ft/16 m high, as part of the preparations for the Bon Festival.

Below: Statue of Arhat Pindola, a monk who is said to have dabbled in the occult, which is why he has to remain outside the temple, seated on a throne-like chair. The statue is touched by visitors for its healing properties.

statue of Vairocana. Legend has it that 2.5 million people were involved in the creation of this statue. This is the equivalent of half the population of Japan at the time and, therefore, seems somewhat unlikely. By the time the Buddha was completed in 751, it had used up almost all of Japan's bronze. The mighty statue was eventually dedicated in a large-scale ceremony in 752. In addition to the imperial family, the ambassadors of China, India, and various other Asian realms were present, as well as hundreds of monks. The highlight of the ceremony was the "opening of the eyes," when an Indian priest standing on a scaffold painted eyes onto the statue using a sacred brush. This brush and the gifts of the illustrious guests can still be viewed in the Shoso-in treasury.

The statue of the Buddha was also damaged in an earthquake and had to be recast. The statue currently on view dates from 1692.

CHINA

The Sacred Mountain of Tai Shan

TAOISM REGARDS THE EARTH AS A LIVING ORGANISM. TAI SHAN, THE MOST
MYSTERIOUS AND SACRED OF TAOISM'S FIVE SACRED MOUNTAINS, IS SAID TO
POSSESS THE GREATEST CONCENTRATION OF ENERGY.

Taoism holds five mountains sacred. Four of them represent the compass points, and the fifth marks the center. According to Chinese mythology, the five peaks were the head and limbs of Pangu, the earth's first living creature, who emerged out of the primeval matter as a result of the cosmic principle of yin and yang. After his death, Pangu's eyes became the sun and the moon, his breath became the wind, and his body became the earth. Tai Shan is located in the Yellow River valley in the province of Shandong, the cradle of Chinese culture. This "Chinese Mount

The Sacred
Mountain of
Tai Shan

Olympus," as it was described by the German pastor and missionary Richard Wilhelm in his 1926 book, *The Soul of China*, is China's most important shrine. As the center of Taoist faith, it lies at the frontier between the Known and the Unknown.

Rigorous and worldly. Taoism goes back to the teachings of the two masters Zhuangzi and Laozi in the fourth century BC. The second of these, author of the *Daodejing* (*Way of Power*, often written as *Tao Te Ching*), is regarded as the true pioneer of this philosophy and religion. Taoism is simultaneously the most rigorous and most worldly doctrine of the path of virtue, for it preached peace, harmony, and understanding of the

FACT FILE

Tai Shan is one of the most climbed mountains in the world. Record year: 2003, when over six million people made the ascent.
Location
Shandong Province in the east of the People's Republic of China.
Height:
5,069 ft/1,545 m—ascent via 6,293 steps or cableway; distance climbed: 4,429 ft/1,350 m.
1987
Inscribed as a UNESCO World Heritage Site.

inner and outer worlds at a time of constant warfare. All confrontation, it maintained, was the consequence of an inability to live in harmony with the true nature of reality—the Tao. "The Tao is something hidden, which no name can describe"; "it is called the face of the faceless, the image of the imageless"; "approach it and you cannot see it; follow it and you cannot see its end." The leading practitioners of this mysterious philosophy developed into masters of alchemy and prediction.

The path is the goal. Over 6,000 steps lead up from the mountain's lowest temple—dedicated to the mountain god—to the Temple of the Jade Emperor (Lord of the Present and Taoism's supreme deity) at the summit. However, before reaching the top via the 5½-mile/9-km flight of steps, visitors encounter along the way numerous smaller temples, springs, cypress groves, waterfalls, lakes, resting places, prayer stops, and places to leave offerings. Taoism teaches that each of its countless gods is omnipresent during the approach to the summit. As a consequence, pilgrims leave offerings to them and pray to them along the entire length of the ascent, for the path is the goal.

Left-hand page: After climbing 6,293 steps, pilgrims eventually reach the Temple of the Jade Emperor at the summit of Tai Shan.

Right: The route to the summit is dotted with prayer stelae, where banknotes are symbolically burned and prayers offered.

Potala Palace

THE ENORMOUS POTALA PALACE IN LHASA, TIBET, IS A SYMBOL OF BOTH SACRED AND SECULAR POWER. UNTIL 1959, IT WAS THE RESIDENCE OF THE DALAI LAMA, THE POLITICAL AND SPIRITUAL LEADER OF TIBET.

A palace was constructed by King Songtsen Gampo of Tibet (reigned AD 617–49) approximately 430 ft/130 m above the city of Lhasa on the 12,139-ft/3,700-m Mar-po-ri (meaning "red mountain") as early as 637. In the seventeenth century, the Fifth Dalai Lama built a new palace over the foundations of the original one to serve as the dwelling of Bodhisattva Avalokiteshvara of the Pure Land of Dewachen. In Tibetan Buddhism, a bodhisattva is one who strives for the highest level of enlightenment and places his "perfection virtue" at the service of all living creatures. As the "Bodhisattva of Universal Compassion," Avalokiteshvara is the patron deity of Tibet. His incarnation on earth is the Dalai Lama. The Potala Palace is still regarded as the holiest place in Tibetan Buddhism and although now only a museum, it remains the most important place of pilgrimage for Tibetan Buddhists.

The White and Red palaces. The palace was constructed in two phases. The first part to be completed was the 11-story Portrang Karpo, or White Palace, which is the seat of government and therefore the secular part of the palace (1653). The 13 stories of the Portrang Marpo, or Red Palace—the sacred part of the palace, which also

Potala Palace

FACT FILE

Lhasa
The capital of the "Autonomous Region of Tibet" (as the region is officially known in the People's Republic of China) lies on the northern edge of the Himalayas. Since 1950, when Lhasa had some 25,000 inhabitants plus 20,000 monks in the city and surrounding monasteries, the population has exploded and now totals 475,000.

Potala Palace
The total surface area of the Potala Palace is approximately 155,500 sq yd/130,000 sq m comprising 999 rooms; the ceilings are supported by 15,000 columns. Approximately 8,160 lb/ 3,700 kg of gold were used in the tomb of the Fifth Dalai Lama.

1994
Inscribed as a UNESCO World Heritage Site.

Left-hand page: The Potala Palace, which perches approximately 430 ft/ 130 m above the city of Lhasa, is still regarded as the most sacred site of Tibetan Buddhism.

Right: A gilded Tibetan Buddha statue, symbolizing perfection of virtue.

includes the Dalai Lama's lodgings—were finished in 1694. The Dalai Lama known as the "Great Fifth" died in 1682, but his death was kept secret for 12 years so as not to endanger the completion of the palace.

Inside the Potala Palace are living rooms, prayer rooms, meditation halls, and temples. Its sheer size is due to the fact that large numbers of monks lived there, as well as the Dalai Lama.

"Autonomous region" of Tibet? In 1959, Chinese troops occupied Tibet and declared it Chinese sovereign territory. The 14th Dalai Lama, the monk Tenzin Gyatso, left Tibet and has been working peacefully ever since toward its independence from China. Tibet may have been transformed by 50 years of Chinese occupation and an intensive settlement policy, but it has not yet been robbed of its cultural identity.

Below: Pilgrims completing the ritual walk around the perimeter of the Potala Palace. Thousands of prayer wheels line the way.

CHINA/TIBET

Sacred Mount Kailash

KANG RINPOCHE, THE TIBETAN NAME OF THIS SACRED PEAK IN THE HIMALAYAS, MEANS "PRECIOUS JEWEL OF SNOWS." PILGRIMS HAVE BEEN COMING HERE TO CIRCUMAMBULATE THE MOUNTAIN FOR OVER 1,000 YEARS.

Mount Kailash

For over a billion followers of four Asian religions, Mount Kailash and the surrounding area is a place of great holiness and a symbol of religious power. For Tibetan Buddhists, it is the center of the universe. For the Bön faithful who practice the traditional religion of Tibet, it represents the very soul of their land. For Hindus, it is the throne of the god Shiva and his consort, Parvati. Finally, for adherents of the Indian religion Jainism, it is the place where Mahavira (circa 599–527 BC), the founder of their faith, attained enlightenment. In ancient Buddhist scriptures and Sanskrit texts, Kailash Meru is described as the "navel of the world" and the axis of the world system.

Reaching for the gods. The pilgrim's way stretches for 33 miles/53 km and is, on average, 16,400 ft/5,000 m high. The going is extremely difficult—not only because of the thinner oxygen at this altitude but also, and most importantly, because of the harsh weather conditions. Nevertheless, thousands of faithful make the three- to four-day pilgrimage each year. In the absolute quiet of the Himalayas, clutching their prayer beads and reciting the mantra "om mani padme hum," the pilgrims feel closer to the gods than would be possible anywhere else

FACT FILE

The height of Mount Kailash, which is located in the Himalayas in Tibet, is 22,028 ft/6,714 m. The mountain has never been climbed. Reinhold Messner was invited by the Chinese government to become the first to do so, but he declined with the words, "One should not trample in mountain boots on gods turned to stone."

Left-hand page: Chiu Monastery, which is by Manasarovar Lake and south of Mount Kailash, is the birthplace of Tibetan Buddhism.

Right: Pilgrims complete a 33-mile/53-km circuit of the mountain in three to four days.

on earth. The climax of the pilgrimage is the crossing of the approximately 18,375 ft/5,600 m-high Dölma La Pass, for after this, pilgrims experience a symbolic death, leaving their old selves behind in the form of hair, drops of blood, or an item of clothing and undergoing a ritual rebirth.

Some devout followers of the Bön religion make full body prostrations along the entire route of the pilgrim's way, taking at least three weeks to complete the circuit. Step, mantra, step. The main time of year for making the circuit is during the fourth month of the Tibetan calendar—in particular, the fifteenth day, when the Saga Dawa Festival is celebrated. This commemorates the day 2,500 years ago on which Shakyamuni (Siddhartha Gautama), the founder of Indian Buddhism, attained nirvana and became a Buddha.

Below: Prayer flags on the famous Tarboche flag mast, which stands over 80 ft/25 m tall. The Buddhist Saga Dawa Festival is held here each year.

The Sacred Ganges River

IN CLOSE PROXIMITY TO EACH OTHER ON THE BANKS OF THE GANGES RIVER ARE TWO OF THE MOST IMPORTANT SACRED SITES OF TWO MAJOR RELIGIONS: THE HINDU TEMPLE OF SHIVA IN VARANASI (BENARES), AND SARNATH, WHERE THE BUDDHA PREACHED FOR THE FIRST TIME.

The Ganges River is sacred to most of India's religions; so, too, are many of the places along its shores. Varanasi (Benares) is sacred to the Hindus and is one of India's seven holy cities. It is believed that the waters of the holy river will wash away all sins, and Hindus are expected to bathe in it at least once in their lives. Many seek to die by the river so that their ashes can be scattered on it. Hindus believe the god Shiva whispers a mantra into the ear of everyone who dies by the river that will preserve them from further reincarnation and guarantee them a lasting place in *swarg* (paradise).

The practice of scattering the ashes of the deceased in the river—which, in extreme cases, can result in half-burned bodies being cast into the water—is becoming an ever greater ecological problem. As a result, authorities have banned the burning of bodies on the ghats, the stone steps that line the riverbanks so that people can bathe in the water. The holiest place in Varanasi is the Temple of Shiva, the god of yogis and wandering monks. This is one of 12 *jyotirlingas*—or shrines—to the supreme god that are scattered throughout India. The jyotirlingas take their name from Shiva's manifestation of himself as a column of light. This aspect of him is worshipped in the form of the lingam—a phallic stone.

The Ganges River

FACT FILE: VARANASI

Fifteenth century
Temple destroyed by
Sultan Sikander Lodi, who
had mosques erected on
the ruins.
Seventeenth century
Temple destroyed by
Aurangzeb, Great
Mogul of India.
1776
Construction of the current
temple by Maharani
Ahalya Bai.
1835
Gilding of the dome with ap-
proximately 1 ton/1 tonne.
of gold by Maharaja Ranjit
Singh, a Sikh king from
the Punjab.

Left-hand page: Varanasi (Benares), the Hindu holy city on the banks of the Ganges, is one of northern India's most important cultural centers.

Right: The entrance to the Durga Temple is decorated on either side with paintings of the many-armed goddess riding a tiger.

The first rotation of the dharma wheel. Just 4 miles/7 km from Varanasi is one of Buddhism's holiest sites: Sarnath, where the Buddha first preached after attaining awakening. This sermon is regarded as the first rotation of the dharma wheel (teaching of the Buddha). It is called the Dhammacakkhapavathana Sutta and led to the founding of the order of itinerant monks known as the *sangha*. Thanks to its proximity to prosperous Varanasi, Buddhism flourished in Sarnath over the following centuries. In the third century AD, Sarnath developed into a major center of Buddhist art, and by the seventh century, it was home to 30,000 monks living in 30 monasteries. At the end of the twelfth century, Sarnath was sacked by the Turks and abandoned until 1836. On the spot where the Buddha is supposed to have preached his first sermon stand the ruins of Dharmekh Stupa, dating from the second century BC. With a diameter of 98 ft/30 m and a height of 131 ft/ 40 m, it bears impressive testimony to past glories.

FACT FILE: SARNATH

Fourth–sixth centuries AD
Golden age during the
Gupta period.
1836
Excavations and restoration
carried out by the British.
Sarnath Archaeological
Museum contains some of
the most important
treasures of Buddhist art,
including the lion capital of
Emperor Ashoka's memorial
pillar, dating from the
third century.

Left: The Buddha lived in Sarnath and, after attaining enlightenment, preached his first sermon here.

INDIA

Bodh Gaya

NOW A TOWN OF OVER 30,000 INHABITANTS, BODH GAYA HAS BEEN INDIA'S MOST IMPORTANT PLACE OF BUDDHIST PILGRIMAGE FOR CENTURIES. DURING THE PERIOD WHEN THE BUDDHA ATTAINED AWAKENING UNDER A TREE HERE, THIS PLACE IN NORTHEAST INDIA WAS KNOWN AS URUVELA.

The botanical name of the Bodhi tree (meaning "tree of awakening"), a relative of the fig, is *Ficus religiosa*. A descendant of the Bodhi tree under which Siddhartha Gautama found enlightenment 2,500 years ago (thereby becoming the Buddha) is venerated here in Bodh Gaya as the most sacred Buddhist shrine. Immediately next to the tree stands Mahabodhi Temple.

According to Buddhist mythology, Siddhartha arrived at the Bodhi tree after years of ascetic living. He sat down in its shade and decided not to leave the

spot until he had attained enlightenment. After 49 days and endless wrestling with Mara (the Buddhist principle of evil—a tempter who tries to arouse craving and desire in those who seek salvation), he finally achieved his goal. The Buddha spent another week in meditation before beginning to walk slowly around the tree in a meditative state.

In the third century BC, Sanghamitta, the daughter of Emperor Ashoka (India's first Buddhist ruler), took a cutting of the Bodhi tree to Sri Lanka and planted it in Anuradhapura, where it still grows (*see p 178*).

Legend has it that Ashoka's wife destroyed the original tree out of anger because she begrudged the time

FACT FILE

It is not known exactly when the Buddha was born or when he died, but Siddhartha Gautama is nevertheless regarded as a historical figure who lived in India in the fifth or sixth century BC.
1891
Founding of the Mahabodhi Society, whose aim was to regain Buddhist control of Bodh Gaya, which had hitherto been in Hindu hands.
1949
Passing of the Bodh Gaya Act, recognizing the place as a Buddhist shrine.
2002
Inscribed as a UNESCO World Heritage Site.

Left-hand page: In front of the Bodhi tree stands a small altar bearing images of Hindu gods, because the Hindus regard the Buddha as an incarnation of Vishnu.

Below: A Buddhist pilgrim by the old stupas of Mahabodhi Temple, next to the sacred tree.

Right: A Buddhist monk at prayer in front of the sacred Bodhi tree beneath which Siddhartha Gautama attained enlightenment in 528 BC.

her husband spent in its shade. Today, each Buddhist monastery contains a Bodhi tree as a symbol of dharma, the universal truths proclaimed by the Buddha.

Center of the world. For the Buddhist faithful, the Bodhi tree and Mahabodhi Temple are the center of the world and the place at which all Buddhas attain awakening. In early Buddhist art, before the Buddha's image became widespread, a tree was used as a symbol of holiness. The tree and temple are visited each year by millions of Buddhists and Hindus (who regard the Buddha as an incarnation of Vishnu). In the third century BC, Emperor Ashoka erected a pillar with an elephant capital next to the tree. Over the following centuries, a wall was built around the pillar and a small temple was constructed within the enclosure. The temple acquired its current form in the second century AD, although it became dilapidated at some point after the eleventh century and was rebuilt by Burmese Buddhists in 1882. The temple is one of the oldest of all Buddhist brick buildings.

The Ajanta and Ellora Caves

FOR A PERIOD OF OVER 900 YEARS, BUDDHIST, HINDU, AND JAINIST MONASTERIES AND TEMPLES WERE CONSTRUCTED IN OVER 60 CAVES AT TWO HOLY SITES IN THE NORTHEAST OF THE INDIAN FEDERAL STATE OF MAHARASHTRA.

The Ajanta Caves. Between the second century BC and the fifth century AD, cave temples and monasteries were constructed as places of Buddhist prayer and meditation in the steep banks of the Waghore River, which rise to a height of just under 265 ft/80 m some 60 miles/ 100 km north of the city of Aurangabad. Their magnificent wall paintings display a far greater level of artistic and technical sophistication than anything produced in Europe at the same time. These holy Buddhist sites were first mentioned by the Chinese pilgrim Hiuen Tsang, who

The Ajanta and Ellora Caves

visited India between AD 629 and 645. For over 1,000 years, Ajanta and its illustrated history of Buddhism in frescoes lay abandoned and covered by the jungle, until British officer John Smith happened upon the caves during a hunting expedition in 1819. Unfortunately, their discovery was extremely harmful to the unique frescoes because hundreds of treasure seekers and amateur archaeologists came to the caves and sliced away sections of the walls at random.

The Ellora Caves. Of the 34 caves at Ellora, only 12 are Buddhist. Of the remaining 22, 17 are Hindu and five are Jainist. Jainism is an Indian religion that emerged in the sixth/fifth century BC and now has just four

FACT FILE

Ajanta
Average size of the caves:
98 × 49 × 13 ft/30 ×
15 × 4 m
Average construction time:
30 years.

Ellora
AD **400–800:** Buddhist caves
are the oldest.
600–900: Hindu temples
are built.
800–1000: Jainist caves are
the least ancient.
Extending approximately
151 ft/46 m into the
cliffside, Kailasa Temple
is the biggest. In order to
create it, between 165,000
tons/150,000 tonnes and
220,000 tons/200,000
tonnes of rock had to
be shifted.

1983
Both complexes inscribed
as UNESCO World
Heritage sites.

Left-hand page: Over the course of some seven centuries, dozens of monasteries and cave temples containing unique frescoes were hewn into the Ajanta cliffsides.

Right: A fresco of Bodhisattva Padmapani in Ajanta. After the discovery of the caves in 1819, many of the frescoes were damaged by treasure hunters.

million or so followers. The Ellora cave shrines were constructed between AD 400 and 700, which makes them less ancient than those of Ajanta. They are located about 19 miles/30 km north of Aurangabad. The cave temples have magnificent facades, outstanding examples of Indian stonemasonry, whose creators were probably well aware of their artistic value. Cave number ten, for example, is dedicated to Vishvakarma, the god of Indian craftspeople. With its sitting Buddha under a stupa, this is both a *chaitya* (in other words, a two-story prayer and meditation center) and a *vihara*, or monastery for itinerant monks.

Below: Kailasa Temple at Ellora (dating from the eighth century AD), whose decoration culminates in a representation of the summit of Mount Kailash, the abode of Shiva in the Himalayas.

Mahabalipuram

HUMAN BEINGS, ANIMALS, GODS, AND SAINTS—ALL ARE REPRESENTED IN A SPIRIT
OF LOVE AND MUTUAL RESPECT ON THE WORLD'S LARGEST SCULPTURAL RELIEF
MYTHOLOGIZING THE GANGES RIVER. IT IS A HINDU VISION OF PARADISE IN PERFECT
AESTHETIC HARMONY.

Fourteen hundred years ago, the rocky landscape south of Chennai (Madras) was transformed into a unique city of temples. For more than 200 years, generations of stonemasons worked the hard granite into breathtakingly beautiful temples. At that time, Mahabalipuram was not the sleepy little town it is today but a major communications center. Extensive canal systems linked villages and towns with the busy port on the Bay of Bengal. Mahabalipuram continues to attract pilgrims from all over the world today. Its exquisite ancient temples are not

museums but a testament to religious faith that is still very much alive.

A signpost to redemption. King Narasimhavaram I (AD 630–66) of the Pallava dynasty, who was renowned for his piety, wanted to unite in one place all the different branches of religion and architectural styles. To this end, he had numerous cave temples cut from the rock. The most unusual of these is the Seven Monoliths Temple. Because of their similarity to the processional chariots that were once dragged through the streets during religious festivals, the rock-hewn temples are known as *rathas*. The Temple of Durga, the goddess of bravery and war, stands next to that of Shiva, her companion, each exhibiting a

FACT FILE

AD 630–60
Construction started at
Mahabalipuram.
690–715
Construction of
Shore Temple under
Narasimhavaram II, or
Rajasimha. The relief
measures 105 × 46 ft/
32 × 14 m and is
also known as
"Arjuna's Penance."
1984
Inscribed as a UNESCO
World Heritage Site.

Left-hand page: The rathas, or rock temples, south of Chennai unite all the religious movements and architectural styles of the day (around AD 600).

Right: Shiva is often shown dancing on Apasmara, the demon of ignorance. In so doing, he destroys uncertainty and creates the universe anew.

typically Hindu opulence. The god himself is depicted leaning against his mount and guardian creature, the bull Nandi, who is also a symbol of the fertility of his master. Behind this temple sits King Narasimhavaram, enthroned on an elephant and surrounded by his wives. Inscriptions acclaim him as the lord of the world. For 1,400 years, there has been a constant flow of pilgrims to Mahabalipuram. These visitors stroke the trunk of the elephant that stands on guard outside one of the temples and touch their hands to their lips. Here, religion is lived and breathed day in and day out. The Pallava dynasty lasted for around 200 years before Mahabalipuram started to decline into the quiet provincial town it has now become. The temples and the relief, however, remain an inspired animated abode of the gods and a signpost to redemption.

Below: The Shore Temple at Mahabalipuram was built in the eighth century and looks out across the Bay of Bengal.

Brihadisvara Temple in Thanjavur

THE TEMPLE COMPLEX IN THANJAVUR HAS STOOD FOR OVER 1,000 YEARS.
ORIGINALLY HAVING THE ASPECT OF A FORTRESS WITH A WALL APPROXIMATELY
40 FT/12 M HIGH, IT IS TODAY ONE OF THE MOST IMPORTANT PLACES OF HINDU
PILGRIMAGE IN INDIA.

Brihadisvara
Temple

In the early eleventh century, King Rajaraja, the ruler of the Chola Empire who extended his sphere of influence to Bengal and Indonesia, built a temple of unbelievable size and beauty in his capital, Thanjavur, some 220 miles/350 km south of present-day Chennai. He dedicated the temple to the god Shiva. Within the context of the Hindu trinity of gods, Shiva is the destroyer, while Brahma is the creator and Vishnu the preserver. Outside this trinity, however, Shiva symbolizes new beginnings and creation, as well as destruction, and bears the epithet, "the Auspicious."

Shiva is also the god of dancers, lust for life, pleasure, and passion. He is usually depicted in the company of his beautiful consort, Parvati. As an embodiment of creation and regeneration, Shiva is also worshipped in the form of the phallus. For this reason, some 1,000 lingams, or phallic shrines, before which the faithful pray, are located in the colonnades around the temple complex. In Hinduism, piety and eroticism are closely intertwined.

The monumental temple was erected in just six years. There is a view north toward the Himalayas, where Shiva sits enthroned on the holy Mount Kailash. The richly decorated central temple tower, a colossal lingam 210 ft/64 m high and constructed of granite blocks, is

Above: The 210-ft/64-m tower of the temple, a lingam built of granite blocks, is known as a vimana.

Above right: Shiva, the god of dancers, pleasure, passion, and lust for life, depicted on a wall of the temple dedicated to him.

Below right: This fresco at Brihadisvara Temple depicts Ganesha, the elephant-headed god of success and son of Shiva.

known as a *vimana*. It is among the tallest of its kind in the world. On the outside wall of the tower is a depiction of the Buddha, who is revered by Hindus as an incarnation of Vishnu. Elsewhere, there is a Christ figure, possibly added by a missionary and taken up by Hinduism.

Slave girls of the gods. Hinduism is no religion for religious fanatics: On the one hand, it focuses on quiet meditation and prayer, and on the other on unbounded and colorful zest for life. During its heyday, the temple maintained 400 dancers known as *devadasis* ("slave girls of the gods"), who served the Hindu faithful and priests as ritual prostitutes. Currently, dancing only occurs during the major festivals. The devadasis no longer exist here, since devout Hindus no longer consider it desirable to send their firstborn daughters to serve in the temple. However, all other traditions remain as lively as ever at the 1,000-year-old temple of Shiva.

FACT FILE

AD 985–1012
Reign of King Rajaraja of the Chola Empire.
1003–10
Construction of the temple complex.
From 1855
Thanjavur comes under direct colonial rule by the British.
1987
Inscribed as a UNESCO World Heritage Site.

The Golden Temple of Amritsar

THE HARMANDIR SAHIB, OR GOLDEN TEMPLE, OF AMRITSAR IN THE PUNJAB IN NORTHERN INDIA IS THE HOLIEST SHRINE OF THE SIKHS AND THE MOST IMPORTANT PLACE OF PILGRIMAGE OF THIS MONOTHEISTIC RELIGION THAT WAS ONLY FOUNDED IN THE FIFTEENTH CENTURY.

Life is an endless learning process, and *Sikh* appropriately means "student." Practicing Sikhs can be recognized by their elaborately tied turbans, covering hair that is never cut. The Sikhs worship a god of creation who is formless and genderless. Priests, monks, and nuns are regarded as unnecessary because individuals are thought to contain the holy within themselves, rendering intermediaries between god and humankind unnecessary. All that counts is to lead a good and virtuous life. Sikhism was founded in the fifteenth century by Guru Nanak (1469–1539) and is therefore a young monotheistic religion.

All people are equal. Construction of the Golden Temple began in 1574, although embellishments, additions, and repairs have been carried out almost continually over the centuries, not least as a result of damage caused during a number of attacks by Muslims. The holy temples of the Sikhs are open to everyone. In Amritsar, this is symbolized by four entrances—which are never closed—facing north, south, east, and west. The only stipulations regarding entry to Sikh shrines are that heads must be covered, and no meat, alcohol, nicotine, or other drugs may be consumed. Maharaja

The Golden Temple of Amritsar

FACT FILE

1574
Land donated for the temple
by Emperor Akbar.
1601
Completion of the temple.
1780–1839
Life of Maharaja Ranjit
Singh, the "Lion of
the Punjab."
2005
Temple renamed
Harmandir Sahib.

Right: Sikh priests before
the Guru Granth Sahib, the
Sikh holy book, in Amritsar
during the Jalau ceremony
to celebrate the 343rd
anniversary of the birth of
the tenth Sikh guru, Guru
Gobind Singh.

Ranjit Singh—the "Lion of the Punjab," as this legendary first Sikh king of a united Punjab was known—endowed the temple with the most precious of materials.

This temple is the main shrine in Amritsar. It sits in the middle of the Amrit Sarovar (meaning "pool of nectar"), a lake fed by an underground spring, on the shore of which the Buddha is believed to have meditated 2,500 years ago. The shrine is reached via the Guru's Bridge, which is a symbol of the journey made by the soul after death. Each evening, the Guru Granth Sahib, the holy book of the Sikhs, is carried over the bridge in procession and laid to rest in its "bed" in the Sikh parliament.

The temple complex has a dining room known as the Guru-ka-Langar in which thousands of people are fed free of charge every day. Regardless of creed, wealth, or social status, the diners sit down to eat together as a symbol of equality before their god. There are also over 400 pilgrims' lodgings at the temple.

Massacre. In 1984, Indira Gandhi (the prime minister at the time) ordered an assault on armed Sikhs who had barricaded themselves in the Golden Temple. Five hundred people were killed. The prime minister was assassinated in retaliation four months later by her two Sikh bodyguards, an event that resulted in another massacre in which, this time, thousands lost their lives.

Left-hand page: Amrit
Sarovar, the lake fed by an
underground spring in the
middle of which sits the
Golden Temple of Amritsar,
means "pool of nectar."

Right: The Sikh holy book
is called the Guru Granth
Sahib. It is carried in
procession over the Guru's
Bridge to the Sikh
parliament each evening.

MYANMAR

Bagan

OVER 2,500 TEMPLES AND PAGODAS SURVIVE IN BAGAN, THE "CITY OF A MILLION PAGODAS," ON THE IRRAWADDY RIVER. ANANDA PAHTO WAS THE FIRST TEMPLE TO BE CONSTRUCTED ON THE PLAIN, AND THE GOLDEN SHWEZIGON PAGODA IS ONE OF MYANMAR'S MOST IMPORTANT RELIGIOUS SITES.

Between the eleventh and thirteenth centuries, Bagan was the capital of the ancient kingdom of Burma and filled the river plain with more than 4,000 temples in order to demonstrate its devotion to the gods. The first of the large temples—and also one of the most beautiful—Ananda Pahto, is located immediately outside the city gates. Its design under King Kyanzittha (reigned 1084–1113) was inspired by eight Indian monks who told the king tales of their life in Nanadamula Cave, a grotto in the Himalayas that is steeped in legend. Ananda Temple

Bagan

was built as a copy of the cave and a reflection of the Buddha's omniscience. Because the Ananda was always a monastery, too, it also includes monks' accommodations within its precincts. The temple is decorated with 80 sandstone reliefs depicting the life of the Buddha from birth to awakening. The temple was restored during the Konbaung era in the late eighteenth century, and to celebrate its nine-hundredth anniversary, its towers were gilded in 1990 and now appear in all their former glory.

Shwezigon Paya. This golden pagoda is Myanmar's most important religious building. As a model for later stupas throughout the country, it marks the turning point from Burma's pre-Buddhist religions to Buddhism.

FACT FILE

Ananda Pahto
Completed 1090.
Square inner courtyard
Length of sides:
174 ft/53 m
Average height:
34 ft/10.5 m
Height of central tower:
167 ft/51 m

Shwezigon Paya
Completed between
1086 and 1090.
1551–81
Major renovation following
an earthquake.
November/December
(Burmese month of Nadaw):
Shwezigon Festival.

1975
Both temples badly
damaged in an earthquake.

Left-hand page: When Bagan was the capital of the Burmese kingdom in the thirteenth century, over 4,000 temples stood on the plains of the Irrawaddy River.

Above left: Gilded statue of the Buddha in Ananda Temple, completed in 1090.

Above right: The golden Shwezigon Pagoda is the most important piece of architecture of the ancient Burmese kingdom. It was erected as Buddhism was emerging in Burma.

Legend has it that the precise location of the shrine was chosen by a white elephant. Construction began in the eleventh century under King Anawrahta (reigned 1044–77), but only three of the temple terraces had been completed when the king was killed by a wild buffalo. The Shwezigon was a monumental shrine for various relics, including the Buddha's frontal bone and a clavicle, a copy of the Buddha's tooth relic kept at Kandy (*see p 182*), and a Chinese emerald Buddha. Of great significance to the history of the Shwezigon was the gift of 37 *nats* ("spirits") by King Anawrahta, which represent a link between the country's traditional religions and Buddhism. The king installed 37 nat figures that were later housed in a room known as the "37 Nats." This is now regarded by pilgrims as one of the most sacred rooms in the temple. Sadly, the figures now on display are copies because the originals have been stolen.

Right: Buddhist monks and novices standing in line for alms and food near Ananda Temple.

LAOS

Luang Prabang

THE HOLY CITY OF LUANG PRABANG IS LOCATED ON THE BANKS OF THE MEKONG
RIVER IN THE MOUNTAINS OF LAOS. FOR CENTURIES, IT WAS THE CAPITAL OF THE
KINGS OF LAOS AND THE CENTER OF LAOTIAN BUDDHISM.

Buddhism continues to dictate the rhythm of life in what is now a small town of just 12,000 people that is surrounded by jungle on the Mekong River. The town has 32 districts, each of which has its own wat, or Buddhist monastery complex. Although the monks are ordained and gather for prayer in the central district, Sim, they live in the individual wats, which also have their own stupas containing immured relics and a "drum tower." Drum towers are designed for religious ceremonies but also serve as meeting rooms in which

issues of local municipal import are discussed. The name comes from the drum that is beaten to summon residents for a meeting. Early each morning, the streets of Luang Prabang are filled with the town's 700 monks and novices requesting and receiving (as a matter of course) their daily bread from the faithful, a sign of how closely town and religion are related. Further evidence of this close relationship is the way the town's sacred places rub shoulders with its private dwellings. In this important center of Buddhist art, culture, and learning, there is no real division between the spiritual and the secular.

Spared by war. Wat Manolom is the oldest temple in Luang Prabang. It is thought to date back to King

Fa Ngum, who united the country in the fourteenth century and introduced Hinayana Buddhism, the older of the two main Buddhist schools. It was here that he had himself crowned the first king of Laos. The facades and gates of the temple are decorated with golden reliefs depicting scenes from the life of the Buddha and telling of the flourishing "kingdom of a million elephants." The city remained the royal capital into the twentieth century and remains an important religious center today. Repeatedly threatened by its powerful neighbors, the small country has lived in constant danger throughout its history. At the end of the nineteenth century, the French subjected Laos to colonial rule. Fortunately, the city was by and large spared the horror of the ensuing wars, and the Communist rulers who later took over have failed to suppress religion. Today, the monks continue to dominate the life of their holy city just as they always have.

FACT FILE

1353
Founding of Lan Xang, the "kingdom of a million elephants."
Since 1356
A place of pilgrimage.
1707
Division of the kingdom into three parts: Luang Prabang, Vientiane, and Champassak.
1893
Laos becomes a French colony.
1958
Fall of Souvanna Phouma and start of civil war.
1975
End of the monarchy. Laos becomes a democratic people's republic.
1995
Inscribed as a UNESCO World Heritage Site.

Left: A monk leans out of the window. The varied ornamentation of the temple is characterized by its careful detail.

Ayutthaya

IN THE FOURTEENTH CENTURY, THERE EMERGED IN SIAM (PRESENT-DAY THAILAND)
A "BLESSED CITY OF ANGELS AND KINGS," KNOWN TODAY AS AYUTTHAYA. IT WAS
ONE OF THE LARGEST CITIES OF THE MIDDLE AGES AND HAS BEEN THE CAPITAL
OF 33 KINGS.

This holy city is dominated, on the one hand, by its many splendid temples and, on the other, by its statues of the Buddha. There is a legend associated with the biggest of these statues, the Reclining Buddha. The story describes how the Buddha was preaching to a demon who was not listening to him because he could not take him seriously due to the Buddha's small stature. Consequently, the Buddha made himself considerably bigger than he really was, and bigger than the demon, forcing him to listen. From this story is derived the Buddhist

teaching that it is inner greatness rather than external appearance that should command respect.

Magnificent temples and monasteries were built in Ayutthaya, and the bell-shaped towers of their *chedis* (reliquary stupas or pagodas) soar above the city. Even in their present ruined state, these edifices convey a strong sense of their former splendor. Here, everything is holy: Beneath the towers of the chedis and temples, secret chambers once contained the relics of saints and the remains of kings, who were themselves revered as gods. It was believed that men and women, and indeed all living creatures, should be religiously anchored in the world through their ancestors. The *prang* (reliquary

Ayutthaya

Left-hand page: Wat Chai Wattanaram, thought to have been built in 1639 by King Prasat Tong over his mother's cremation site. Two of the many stone Buddha statues can be seen sitting in front of the ruins.

Right: The temples of Ayutthaya are still an important object of pilgrimage for Buddhists, including monks.

tower) of Wat Mahathat, which once stood 164 ft/50 m high, is believed to have formerly housed a relic of the Buddha. This temple and the monastery attached to it once lay at the geographical center of Ayutthaya.

Tears of grief. In the eighteenth century, the city was destroyed by Burmese troops following a two-year siege. The king was toppled, the treasuries were plundered, and the "blessed city of angels and kings" ceased to exist as a holy site. Just over 40 years ago, robbers discovered two chambers inside one of the prangs. They succeeded in making off with most of the treasures, just a few of which were recovered. Another temple, Wat Phanom Choeng, is thought to have existed before Ayutthaya was built. This holy temple has now been completely renovated and still towers over Ayutthaya as a modern emblem of the city. It contains one of the oldest and most beautiful statues of the Buddha in all of Asia: the Great Buddha, which originally stood outside the temple so that it could be seen from far and wide. There is a legend attached to this statue, too: Following the complete destruction of the city by the Burmese in 1767, the Buddha is supposed to have shed tears of grief.

FACT FILE

1350
City of Ayutthaya founded as the capital by King Rama Thibodi.
1350–1767
Kingdom of Ayutthaya.
1492–1532
Construction of reliquaries known as chedis.
1511
Discovery of Siam by the Portuguese.
1767
Destruction by the Burmese.
1956
Start of restoration.
1991
Inscribed as a UNESCO World Heritage Site.

Left: Boats on the river with Wat Chai Wattanaram in the background.

Angkor Wat

NOT FAR FROM THE CITY OF SIEM REAP IS ONE OF THE LARGEST RELIGIOUS ENSEMBLES IN THE WORLD: THE TEMPLE COMPLEX OF ANGKOR WAT, BUILT BY KHMER KING SURYAVARMAN II BETWEEN 1113 AND 1150.

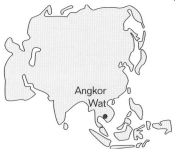

Angkor Wat

Suryavarman II, known as the "protégé of the sun god," had Angkor Wat designed as a reflection on earth of the heavenly cosmos. It was to be his funerary temple and a center of the cult of the Hindu god Vishnu. In harmony with the beliefs and culture of the Khmer people, the temple complex combined the religious with the profane. The entire complex is enclosed by a moat 656 ft/200 m wide. Angkor Wat incorporates the largest religious building in the world—the Heavenly Palace—center of the Khmer realm and, therefore, of the world. Entering through the main gateway, visitors pass into a series of rectangular courtyards, each of which contains a lotus-flower tower. At around 200 ft/60 m high, the central tower symbolizes Mount Meru, regarded as the center of the Hindu universe.

Built by gods and for gods. Given that the Khmer kings regarded themselves as deities, Angkor was seen by the people as having been built by gods and for gods. It was thus the divine architect, Vishnu—the brother of Shiva, and the many-armed ruler of the world and preserver—who had constructed this fantastic complex.

The gallery of the main portal still contains a statue thought to depict King Suryavarman II as Vishnu.

FACT FILE

Ninth–fifteenth centuries AD
Main period of
Khmer culture.
1113–50
Planning and construction
of Angkor Wat in the
southeast district of capital
Yasodharapura under King
Suryavarman II.
Circa 1200
Planning and construction
of the "great royal city" of
Angkor Thom.
1353, 1393, and 1431
Pillaging, plundering, and
eventual abandoning and
decline of the city.
Sixteenth century
Portuguese travelers
discover Angkor Wat.
1860
French explorer
Henri Mouhot discovers
Angkor Wat two years
before his death.
1992
Inscribed as a UNESCO
World Heritage Site.

Left-hand page: Ta Prohm Temple is famous for its thick tree roots. This side of the temple has been left unrestored to show the condition of the complex when it was discovered.

Right: Buddhist monks in front of the Banteay Samre Temple, which forms part of the temple complex of Angkor Wat, center of the Khmer realm and, therefore, the world.

The churning of the sea of milk. One of the temple's stone reliefs depicts the "churning of the sea of milk," an important episode in Hindu mythology. At the heart of this story is the notion of the world as a butter churn filled with milk. The sea of milk is enclosed by three mountains with Mount Meru, the abode of the gods (in other words, Angkor Wat), in the center. The churning stick is Mount Mandara, and the churning rope is the serpent Vasuki. The gods are shown pulling on the left and their enemies on the right. Together, they cause the mountain to gyrate, with the result that the milk of life turns to butter and the vessel discharges an elixir of immortality that confers redemption and eternal life.

Below: The entire temple complex is surrounded by a 656-ft/ 200-m wide moat representing the cosmic ocean. Within is the inhabited world.

Anuradhapura

FOR OVER 1,300 YEARS, THE SACRED CITY OF ANURADHAPURA WAS THE CENTER OF SRI LANKAN CIVILIZATION. ONE OF ITS TREASURES IS THE MONUMENTAL JETAVANARAMA STUPA THAT IS BELIEVED TO CONTAIN A SASH BELONGING TO THE BUDDHA.

Anuradhapura had been inhabited since the tenth century BC, but it was not until the third century BC, when Sanghamitta, the founder of a Buddhist order of nuns, brought with her and planted a cutting of the Bodhi tree (meaning "tree of awakening"), that Anuradhapura became the political and, above all, religious center of the land. At its zenith, the city's influence and colossal proportions were comparable to those of Babylon or Nineveh. Anuradhapura was enclosed by a square city wall and possessed an outstanding irrigation system—one of the most complex in the ancient world. After its destruction in AD 993 by Rajaraja I of the Chola Empire, Anuradhapura was abandoned and gradually became overgrown by the jungle. The ruins include bell-shaped stupas constructed of small air-dried bricks, temples, sculptures, and an ancient drinking-water reservoir. The ruined city was rediscovered in the nineteenth century by British soldiers, and since 1870, its palaces, monasteries, and temples have turned it into a place of pilgrimage for Buddhists all over again.

The Tree of Awakening. The Sri Maha Bodhiya, a peepul tree (*Ficus religiosa*), is one of the oldest living trees in the world. The cutting brought by Sanghamitta

Anuradhapura

Left-hand page and right: Wall of elephants in front of Jetavanarama Dagoba. The elephant is extremely popular on the Indian subcontinent. The young elephant god, Ganesha, appears as a good-luck charm or protector on houses and temples.

from Bodh Gaya around 245 BC was planted on a terrace some 21 ft/6.5 m high and protected by a balustrade. Today, the tree is one of Sri Lanka's holiest relics and is venerated by Buddhists from all over the world. During the reign of King Kirthi Sri Rajasingha, a wall was built around the tree to protect it from wild elephants.

Jetavanarama Dagoba. In the third century AD, King Mahasan (271–301) built one of the world's largest *dagobas* (a form of stupa that developed in Sri Lanka). The Jetavanarama, constructed of air-dried bricks, is around 330 ft/100 m high and was once surrounded by a 7½-acre/ 3-ha compound that accommodated approximately 3,000 monks. Believed to be immured in the shrine is a sash knotted by the Buddha himself, making the dagoba one of the holiest places in Anuradhapura and the entire Buddhist world.

FACT FILE

Location
155 miles/250 km north of the capital, Colombo; city walls approximately 16 miles/26 km long.
Enclosed area: 256 square miles/663 sq km
1679
The first European to set eyes on the holy city was British sea captain Robert Knox (1641–1720).
1982
Inscribed as a UNESCO World Heritage Site.

Far left: Stupas are dome-shaped Buddhist reliquaries. The Mahiyangana Stupa commemorates what is thought to be the first place visited by the Buddha in Sri Lanka.

Left: Ruwanweli Stupa in Anuradhapura was built by King Dutugamunu over 2,200 years ago.

The Sacred Mountain of Sri Pada

AT THE BEGINNING OF EACH YEAR, A MAJOR PILGRIMAGE TO SRI PADA TAKES PLACE. SRI PADA IS A MOUNTAIN SACRED TO THE FAITHFUL OF THREE DIFFERENT RELIGIONS—HINDUISM, BUDDHISM, AND ISLAM.

Sri Pada

Between the end of December and April, the summit of Sri Pada is the destination for thousands of pilgrims. It is the site of a giant footprint some 60 inches/150 cm long and 28 inches/70 cm wide from which the mountain takes its name. For more than a 1,000 years, this mountain peak has been a center of religious practice for three faiths, each of which regards the footprint as holy. However, the mountain had been venerated by Sri Lanka's original inhabitants long before these three religions were present on the island. These indigenous peoples named the mountain Samanala Kanda, Saman being one of the island's four patron deities. The Buddhists, whose history on the island goes back to 300 BC, believe the visible footprint conceals another footprint left by the Buddha on a sapphire on the occasion of his third and last visit to the island.

According to Hindu mythology, the footprint was left by the god Shiva when he performed the dance of creation. The Hindus call the mountain Sivan Adi Padham. The Muslims, meanwhile, venerate the mark as the footprint of Adam, who, according to legend, stood on one leg here when he was cast out of paradise. God sent him to Sri Lanka because the country bore

FACT FILE

Height:
7,359 ft/2,243 m, the island's fourth-highest mountain.

Fourth century BC
Legend has it that the steps and climbing chains were installed by Alexander the Great (356–323 BC).

1292
Marco Polo (1254–1324) visited the mountain and described its pyramidal shape.

Fourteenth century
The Arab explorer Ibn Batuta (1304–68) called Sri Pada the highest mountain in the world.

Left-hand page: The ascent begins at nighttime. The route is dotted with lights and tearooms where the pilgrims can refresh themselves.

Right: The stupa-shaped Japanese Peace Pagoda at the foot of Sri Pada.

the closest resemblance to paradise. Adam is revered as a prophet in Islam.

One step away from paradise. Normally, pilgrims begin to make their way up the mountain at night in order to avoid the heat of the day and enjoy the sunrise. However, the ascent—particularly the shorter northern route—partly via steps and partly assisted by chains fixed into the rock, is not without danger, and injuries and even deaths have occurred. Islanders of all creeds believe the distance from the summit of Sri Pada to paradise to be just 40 miles/65 km and that from the top, it is even possible to hear the murmur of the fountains of paradise. On a platform next to the Temple of Saman, with its large footprint, where the faithful leave offerings, there is a small Buddhist temple with a bell that pilgrims strike after reaching the sacred destination.

Below: A man in prayer before the large footprint in the Temple of Saman, the pilgrims' final destination.

The Temple of the Tooth in Kandy

THE INHABITANTS OF THE ROYAL CITY OF KANDY IN THE HEART OF SRI LANKA USED
TO CALL THEIR HOME KANDA-UDA-PAS-RATA, MEANING "HIDDEN KINGDOM IN THE
MOUNTAINS." IN 1815, WITH LITTLE CONSIDERATION OF LOCAL SENSITIVITIES,
THE BRITISH COLONIAL RULERS CHANGED THE NAME TO KANDY.

Gautama Buddha died in 480 BC, and his body was cremated outside the gates of the city of Kusinara in northern India. According to legend, four teeth and a clavicle were rescued from the Buddha's ashes. While Buddhism was being suppressed by Hinduism, the veneration of these relics met with the disapproval of the ruling Hindus. One of the teeth is supposed to have been smuggled in the hair of a princess across the sea to Sri Lanka, where the Dalada Maligawa, or Temple of the Tooth, was erected in its honor. The tooth is Sri Lanka's most important

The Temple of
the Tooth

Buddhist relic. Not only was it a religious treasure, but it was also closely linked to the royal throne: Only he who had the tooth in his possession could be king. It is for this reason that the temple and palace compounds enjoy such physical proximity to one another in the center of the city. A two-week festival is held each year in honor of the sacred tooth. The Perahera in Kandy is one of the most colorful and magnificent festivals in Asia. Its rituals and ceremonies have changed little over time and demonstrate the power of a living faith. As part of the festivities, hundreds of decorated elephants, dancers, fakirs, musicians, and dignitaries from all over the whole country move in procession through the city.

Left-hand page: A guard inside the Temple of the Tooth. The elephant tusks underline the message that unauthorized persons are not permitted to enter.

Right: The Temple of the Tooth forms part of the royal palace complex. The relic of the Buddha was of special legitimating significance to the Sinhalese royal house.

Desecration by the colonial rulers. For 200 years, the country struggled against colonization by the Dutch, the Portuguese, and the British. There was an ancient belief that the country would remain invincible as long as no road led to Kanda-uda-pas-rata. In 1815, the British crushed the opposition and with it, Sinhalese culture, and desecrated its holiest of holies by removing the tooth from its reliquary. This had never happened before; no one other than the finder of the tooth had ever set eyes upon it. The relic was not returned to the temple until 31 years later. Humiliated, the last Sinhalese king, Sri Vikrama Rajasingha, signed the surrender document on March 2, 1815, in the great audience chamber where the end of colonial rule and the independent republic of Sri Lanka were eventually proclaimed in 1972. Today, the country is a multiethnic and multifaith nation whose other main religions (in addition to Buddhism) are Hinduism, Christianity, and Islam.

FACT FILE

1707–39
Construction of the existing Temple of the Tooth under King Narendrasingha.
1784
Construction of the audience chamber.
1798–1815
Reign of the last king, Sri Vikrama Rajasingha.
1988
Inscribed as a UNESCO World Heritage Site.

Far left and left: The shrine is opened three times a day, when ceremonies are carried out in honor of the Buddha.

Borobudur

THE HOLY SITE OF BOROBUDUR ON JAVA IS A GEM OF BUDDHIST ARCHITECTURE. SYMBOLIZING THE COSMIC MOUNTAIN AT THE CENTER OF THE WORLD, ITS LAVISH SCULPTURAL DECORATION SHOWS THE PATH TO AWAKENING.

Over 1,200 years ago, during the Shailendra dynasty, countless Javanese farmers and craftspeople, under expert direction, erected Buddhism's largest sacred building (a stupa) not far from the city of Yogyakarta. It was completed between AD 760 and 830. Above a square ground plan of 361 × 361 ft/ 110 × 110 m rise five stepped platforms surmounted by a further three circular levels crowned by a stupa. Four flights of steps positioned on the axes lead to the summit of this artificial mountain with cosmic meaning. Those seeking to explain the structure's significance point out its mandala-like design, evident from the ground plan, and 72 smaller crowned stupas, more than 500 statues of the Buddha, and approximately 1,460 relief sculptures. The tripartite structure of the complex is related to the three Buddhist spheres of existence: the realm of desire, the realm of heavenly forms, and the realm of formlessness. Borobudur has also been interpreted as representing Mount Sumeru, the abode of the gods. By repeatedly circumambulating the stupa, passing its many reliefs and gradually ascending to the top through a system of stairways and corridors, pilgrims are led symbolically to life's goal.

Borobudur

FACT FILE

Circa AD 760
Start of construction during
the Shailendra dynasty.
1814
"Rediscovery" of the site by
an English colonial official.
1948
Preliminary research for the
restoration of the complex.
1973
Start of restoration work.
1985
Bomb attack resulting in
damage to nine of
the stupas.
1991
Inscribed as a UNESCO
World Heritage Site.

Below: One of the
72 abbreviated stupas
on the upper terraces at
Borobudur. In each of these
stupas is seated a statue
of the Buddha, indicating
with its hand gestures the
"turning of the wheel
of doctrine."

Left-hand page:
When Borobudur was
"rediscovered" in 1814,
two empty chambers were
found in the central stupa.
It is possible that a relic
of the Buddha was once
kept here.

Right: One of the numerous
reliefs. Borobudur's 1,460
narrative panels depict
different Buddhist scriptures
and point out the path
to awakening.

The path to enlightenment. Research conducted between 1885 and 1938 ascertained that the 1,460 panels of the reliefs depict five different Buddhist scriptures. In order to follow the narrative sequence of the reliefs from beginning to end, pilgrims would have to have circumambulated the monument ten times. The figure ten was by no means chosen at random. It refers to the number of perfections or stages of existence that need to be cultivated by a bodhisattva on the path to awakening. There is significant evidence that Borobudur poses the classic questions pondered by the Buddhist mystic: How does one acquire divine powers, and how does one attain spiritual liberation? Many of the scenes depicted by the reliefs are so lifelike that they have an immediate appeal for those not of the Buddhist religion. To acquire a better understanding of their meaning, however, a guide is advisable—a role no doubt performed at one time by monks.

Borobudur harks back to a time over 1,000 years ago when Buddhism was enjoying a short-lived golden age on Java.

ISRAEL

Jerusalem

JERUSALEM IS ONE OF THE OLDEST CONTINUOUSLY INHABITED SETTLEMENTS IN THE WORLD. THE CITY CONTAINS HOLY SITES OF ENORMOUS SIGNIFICANCE FOR JEWS, CHRISTIANS, AND MUSLIMS, AND HAS BEEN SHAPED BY A LONG HISTORY OF RELIGIOUS, CULTURAL, AND POLITICAL CONFLICT.

The Temple Mount is revered by Jews as a holy place because it was here that King Solomon (the son of King David, who conquered the city in 1003 BC) erected the first temple to house the Ark of the Covenant. To enter the Holy of Holies where the Ark of the Covenant stood was a privilege reserved for the high priests, and to this day, devout Jews refuse to enter the Temple Mount precinct out of reverence for the site where the Holy of Holies was once located. The temple was destroyed by Nebuchadnezzar II (reigned circa 604–562 BC). Work on the second temple, which was later destroyed by Roman troops, began about 520 BC under Zerubbabel. This second temple, which underwent significant reconstruction by King Herod beginning around 21 BC, was the last refuge of the Jews during the Jewish-Roman War and is thought to have been set on fire by them in order to prevent its desecration by the Romans. The latter erected a temple to Jupiter on the site, which was later demolished by Emperor Constantine, a Christian. Justinian I (AD 482–565), who was responsible for Hagia Sophia in Constantinople (*see pp 122–3*), constructed a church on the Temple Mount dedicated to the Virgin Mary. Both his churches suffered the same fate: They were turned into mosques. According to

Left-hand page: The
Western Wall of the former
Jewish second temple is a
much-frequented place
of prayer.

Right: Slips of paper bearing
requests and prayers are
pushed into the cracks
between the large stone
blocks of the wall.

Jewish-Christian tradition, the sacred rock of Muhammad in the Dome of the Rock is the very one on which Abraham was to have sacrificed his son Isaac.

The "Wailing Wall." The most important Jewish shrine remains the western foundation wall of the second temple, which extends for some 1,300 ft/400 m. Since the Six Day War of June 5–10, 1967, the faithful have once more been able to pray at the wall. Previously, this was Jordanian territory and Jews were prohibited from entering it. Due to the body language and gestures with which prayer is sometimes accompanied, the Western Wall is often incorrectly referred to as the "Wailing Wall." Part of the ritual involves inserting slips of paper bearing supplications and prayers into the cracks in the wall.

Christian Jerusalem. The Christians regard Jerusalem's old city and the nearby Mount of Olives as the holy scene of Christ's passion and ascension. The most important site within the old city walls, and one of the most important shrines in the whole of Christendom, is the Church of the Holy Sepulchre, which is venerated by many as the place of Christ's crucifixion and entombment. Today, it is the seat of the Greek Orthodox Patriarch of Jerusalem and the Catholic Archpriest of the Basilica of the Holy Sepulchre.

Below: In addition to various relics associated with the passion of Christ, the Church of the Holy Sepulchre, one of the holiest sites in Christendom, contains the site of Christ's tomb.

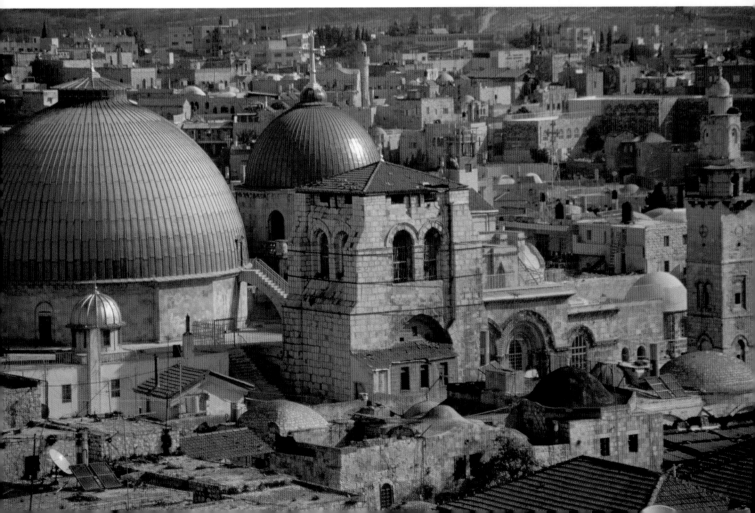

FACT FILE:
CHRISTIAN JERUSALEM

Year 0
The birth of Jesus and the beginning of the Christian calendar.

AD 335
Consecration of the Church of the Holy Sepulchre.

527–65
Golden age of Byzantine Jerusalem.

1887
Construction of the New Gate to provide access to the Christian quarter.

Right: Crucifix-bearing pilgrims move in procession to the Church of the Holy Sepulchre. For Christians, the cross is a symbol of suffering and salvation.

Below: The magnificent Dome of the Rock, with its golden cupola, is the most important Islamic shrine after the holy sites in Mecca and Medina.

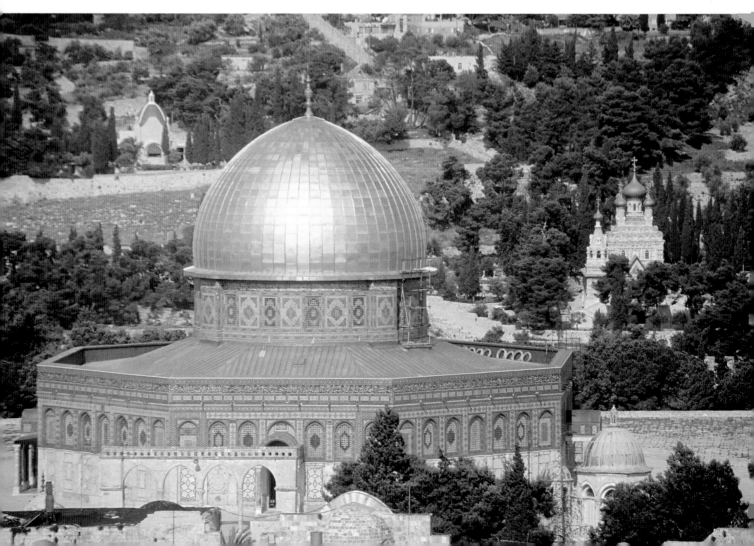

A Christian-Muslim battleground. The Islamic rulers of Jerusalem raised the al-Aqsa Mosque over the demolished Christian Church of Our Lady on the Temple Mount. The Christians who invaded the city during the First Crusade in 1099 instigated a bloodbath, and on the square around the mosque and Dome of the Rock alone over 10,000 people were beheaded. The mosque was demolished and a new church built that from 1119 onward provided quarters for the Knights Templar, founded the same year by Hugues de Payns (1080–1136). In 1187, Sultan Saladin defeated the Crusaders in Egypt, Syria, and Palestine, and the Church of Our Lady was turned back into a mosque. The turbulent history of the mosque remains a cause of religious and political conflict today.

Islamic Jerusalem. Islam venerates the Temple Mount as a holy site because it was from here that Muhammad ascended to heaven. According to legend, Muhammad embarked on his night journey from Mecca to Jerusalem (this journey is called al-Isra) on the divine mount, al-Buraq (meaning "lightning")—a combination of a winged horse and donkey with the face of a woman—on the advice of the archangel Gabriel. There, at the rock of Abraham, he was to meet the prophets of whom he was the latest in the line after Adam, Noah, Abraham, Moses, John, and Jesus. He climbed a ladder of light through the seven heavens all the way to God, who taught him the art of prayer. That same night, Muhammad rode back. His night journey is interpreted as an astral journey, as incorporeal existence, the highest stage of religious devotion.

Muhammad's footprint. Devout Muslims venerate the footprint left by Muhammad in the rock when he climbed to heaven. The rock wanted to follow, but Gabriel held it firm, and consequently, impressions of his handprints were left in it, too. The Dome of the Rock was constructed over the boulder by Khalif Abd al-Malik. The Prophet had chosen this place because, according to tradition, this is where Abraham had wanted to sacrifice his son Isaac. A relic of the Prophet's hair is worshipped at the Dome of the Rock. Devout pilgrims undertake a circumambulation of the shrine.

FACT FILE:
ISLAMIC JERUSALEM

Circa AD 570
Birth of Muhammad
in Mecca.
June 8, 632
Death of Muhammad
in Mecca.
Between 688 and 691
Construction of the
Dome of the Rock
(Masjid Qubbat As-Sakhrah).
1187
Jerusalem conquered by
Saladin's army.
June 1967
Reunification of the city.
1981
Jerusalem inscribed as a
UNESCO World
Heritage Site.

Above right: Muslim women in the Dome of the Rock, built as a shrine over the boulder on which Abraham was to sacrifice his son Isaac.

Right: Christian Orthodox leaders. Ancient traditions play a more important role in the Orthodox Church than in the Roman Church.

Bethlehem

BARELY 6 MILES/10 KM FROM JERUSALEM YET, SINCE 1995, NO LONGER IN ISRAELI TERRITORY, BETHLEHEM IS THE HOME OF KING DAVID AND THE BIRTHPLACE OF JESUS. IT IS ONE OF THE MOST VISITED PLACES OF PILGRIMAGE IN THE WORLD.

Bethlehem has been a place of pilgrimage for Christians since the construction of the Church of the Nativity in the fourth century AD. For nearly as long, the town has had a monastery, built in the fifth century by St. Jerome—the translator of the Bible from Hebrew to Latin. St. Jerome is buried in a cave beneath the Church of the Nativity. Until the arrival of the Crusaders, Bethlehem was a thriving center. Thereafter, its population gradually dwindled. Not until 1948, when thousands of Palestinian refugees arrived, did the town start to revive and

grow again in terms of numbers and importance. Like Jerusalem, Bethlehem is a holy site for three religions. For the Jews, it is the site of the tomb of Rachel, mother of Joseph, one of the patriarchs of the 12 tribes of Israel. The Christians revere Bethlehem as the birthplace of Jesus, while the Prophet Muhammad preached here on his way to Jerusalem, saying, "Gabriel spoke the words: '… here is the place of birth of your brother Jesus. Peace be with him.'"

Church of the Nativity. The Church of the Nativity in Bethlehem is one of Christianity's holiest sites and oldest places of worship. According to the Gospel of St. Luke, Jesus was placed in a manger when

Left-hand page: While the Church of the Holy Sepulchre in Jerusalem is associated with Christ's death and entombment, the Church of the Nativity in Bethlehem is associated with his birth.

Right: On this spot once stood the modest grotto, or cave, in which Christ the Redeemer came into the world.

FACT FILE

AD 327–39
Church of the Nativity built by St. Helen.
530
New church built by Emperor Justinian.
1834
A fire—and in 1869, an earthquake—destroys parts of the interior.
Since 1852
The church has been under the stewardship of the Roman Catholic, Armenian, and Greek Orthodox Churches.
1995
Bethlehem comes under the jurisdiction of the Palestinian government. The name Bethlehem is derived from the Hebrew Beit Lechem, meaning "house of bread."

he was born, leading to the conclusion that a stable (which was often a cave) was where his birth took place. At the beginning of the fourth century, St. Helen, the mother of Emperor Constantine, built a church over the cave. The first church was octagonal and located directly over the cave. At its center was a cavity 13-ft/4-m wide surrounded by railings, allowing people to look down into Christ's place of birth. Parts of the grotto's mosaic floor date from this early period. At the beginning of the sixth century, this first church was destroyed and subsequently rebuilt by Emperor Justinian on a far larger scale. In the cave, the spot purported to be the precise place of birth is marked by a silver star bearing the Latin inscription, "Hic de Virgine Maria Jesus Christus natus est" ("The Virgin Mary here gave birth to Jesus Christ".) Fifteen lamps hang in the grotto, six belonging to the Greek, five to the Armenian, and four to the Catholic Churches. All the other furnishings postdate the earthquake of 1869.

Right: The basilica was not always a haven of peace. In the eighteenth century, there were disputes between the various Christian denominations about how it should be used, and in 2002, it was besieged by Palestinian militiamen.

Ur

UR WAS THE CENTER OF ANCIENT MESOPOTAMIA AND THE OLDEST SUMERIAN CITY. THE FIRST SETTLEMENT IN THIS PLACE WAS FOUNDED AS EARLY AS THE FOURTH OR FIFTH MILLENNIUM BC. UR IS THE SITE OF A ZIGGURAT DEDICATED TO THE MOON GOD NANNA.

Due to the development of an effective irrigation system, the land between the Euphrates and Tigris rivers was rendered cultivatable during the early years of Ur's history (Ubaid period, fifth/fourth millennium BC). Around 2235 BC, the first major empire was forged by King Sargon as a result of numerous conquests in the Akkad region. After the fall of this empire some 200 years later, its territory was taken over by Ur and its Third Dynasty rulers. The city-state soon rose to heights never again achieved. The city worshipped the moon god Nanna as its patron deity and dedicated magnificent cult centers to him.

Ziggurat of the moon god Nanna. The temples and ziggurat dedicated to Nanna stood in a sacred wall-enclosed precinct known as a *temenos*. Nanna was the father of the sun god and of Ishtar. His symbol is a horizontal crescent moon conceived as a boat in which he sails across the heavens.

A temple for the cult of the moon god was begun by King Ur-Nammu and completed by his son Shulgi. The shrine's ziggurat, an Assyrian three-stage structure with thick walls, a height of 82 ft/25 m, and base dimensions of 205 × 141 ft/62.5 × 43 m, was crowned with a sacristy.

FACT FILE

Circa 4000–3500 BC
Ubaid period.
2300–2215 BC
King Sargon of Akkad.
2100 BC
King Ur-Nammu begins
construction of a ziggurat
dedicated to Nanna.
2047–1999 BC
King Shulgi (Ur-Nammu's
son) completes the ziggurat.
2047–1940 BC
Ur takes over the Akkadian
Empire under the rulers of
the Third Dynasty.
AD 1922–34
During excavations by
British archaeologist
Leonard Woolley, most
of the royal tombs are
discovered.

Below: The stepped towers
known as ziggurats provided
the original model for the
biblical idea of the
Tower of Babel.

Left-hand page: A large
flight of steps leading
to the top of the ziggurat.
The word *ziggurat* is of
Babylonian origin.

Right: Relief on a vase,
showing offerings being
made to the god Nanna.

The first stage was 36 ft/11 m high and could be reached via flights of wide steps that met at the top. The top two stories are estimated to have been 18 ft 8 inches/ 5.7 m and 9 ft 6 inches/2.9 m high. The ziggurat represented the symbolic joining of heaven and earth, the fusing of man and god. If a heavenly being wanted to form a union with a member of the human race, it had to descend from heaven to the main temple at the foot of the ziggurat, where the people made offerings to their gods. The appearance of the city was dominated by the temenos and holy temples, while the lives of its inhabitants were dominated by the religious rites.

An important aspect of religious life was the cult of the dead. During the course of excavations, over 2,000 graves were found, some containing more than 70 skeletons. Almost all were from the period circa 2600–2500 BC. Dead royals were accompanied to the next world by a retinue of dignitaries and warriors, who were first stunned and then slaughtered along with the draft animals needed to pull the chariots of the kings and princes.

IRAN, MASHHAD

The Shrine of Imam Reza

MASHHAD, THE CAPITAL OF THE KHORASAN PROVINCE IN NORTHEAST IRAN, IS THE
COUNTRY'S SECOND-LARGEST CITY. IT IS FAMOUS FOR THE SHRINE OF IMAM REZA,
AN EXQUISITELY BEAUTIFUL PLACE OF PILGRIMAGE.

I n the Muslim world, an imam is the leader of a community, the prayer leader in a mosque, or sometimes a great scholar who has been given the title as a sign of respect. For Shiites, the word has a range of meanings: from someone entrusted by God with a mission to the apotheosis of such an individual. Reza was born in Medina in AD 765 and quickly acquired a reputation for great spirituality and enormous wisdom. At the age of 51, he was summoned by Caliph Mamun to Sanabad. Mamun proclaimed Reza his successor and gave him the hand of his

daughter in marriage. Members of the various Shiite sects celebrated this appointment, but the Sunnis rejected it and revolted. Together, Mamun and Reza traveled to Baghdad in order to reconquer the city, but on the way, Reza fell ill and quickly wasted away. His sudden death led the Shiites to suspect he had been poisoned by Mamun in order to appease the rebellious residents of this predominantly Sunni area who had opposed him. However, the caliph grieved sincerely for the imam, and in 818, he built a mausoleum for Reza next to the tomb of his own father, Harun al-Rashid. Because of the persistent suspicion on the part of the Shiites that Mamun had killed Imam Reza, Sanabad soon became a place

The Shrine of
Imam Reza

of pilgrimage, and its name was changed to Mashhad ar-Rizawi, meaning "place of martyrdom of Reza."

Twenty million pilgrims. A legend soon began that one pilgrimage to the shrine of Imam Reza was worth 70,000 pilgrimages to Mecca, and thus the tomb quickly came to be regarded as a holy place, attracting thousands of visitors from the length and breadth of Persia. Toward the end of the tenth century, the shrine was destroyed by Sultan Sabuktagin, but was rebuilt by his son Mahmud of Ghazna just a few years later. At the beginning of the thirteenth century, the Mongols plundered both the mausoleum and city, but about 100 years later, the Mongol ruler Sultan Muhammad Khodabandeh converted to Shiism and had the shrine rebuilt to a state more magnificent than ever.

During the reign of the Safavid kings from 1501 to 1786, under whom Shiism became the official religion, the tomb complex was expanded into a shrine of hitherto unseen splendor, with gilded domes, tiled minarets, and spacious gardens and courtyards. The shrine is one of the seven holy Shiite sites, and today, it consists of two mosques, several *madrasas* (Qur'an schools, or places of Islamic learning), museums housing cultural and artistic treasures, and over 20 other buildings. Every year, more than 20 million Muslims make the pilgrimage to the site.

FACT FILE

AD **818**
Imam Reza dies, and his first mausoleum is built.
993
Destruction of the mausoleum by Sultan Sabuktagin.
1009
Reconstruction by Mahmud of Ghazna.
1220
Destruction by the Mongols.
1304–16
Reign of Sultan Muhammad Khodabandeh.
1912
Russian troops damage the shrine.

Left: Carved stonework and lavish mosaics decorate the large wall with recessed arch in the inner courtyard of the shrine.

SAUDI ARABIA

Mecca

THE PROPHET MUHAMMAD, THE FOUNDER OF ISLAM, WAS BORN IN MECCA AROUND
AD 570. THE CITY IS THE SITE OF THE LARGEST MOSQUE IN THE WORLD: THE AL-HARAM,
OR GRAND MOSQUE, WITH ITS HOLY SHRINE, THE KAABA. MILLIONS OF MUSLIMS
MAKE THE PILGRIMAGE TO THIS MOST SACRED OF ISLAMIC SHRINES EACH YEAR.

It is believed that the Islamic shrine known as the Kaaba was built by Adam, the first prophet. Abraham and his son Ishmael discovered the abandoned building and rebuilt it. Each of these figures plays an important role in Islam, as well as in Christianity and Judaism. The cult of the "Black Stone" has existed in Mecca since pre-Islamic times. Fragments of it are set into the wall of the Kaaba. The Black Stone of the Kaaba is thought to be a meteorite, though this is merely conjecture since to date no geological analysis has ever taken place. According to tradition, Abraham was given the stone by the archangel Gabriel. There is a legend that it was originally white but that it turned black over the course of the centuries out of sorrow over the sins of the world. The al-Haram Mosque, also known as the Grand Mosque, determines the direction of prayer (*qiblah*) of Muslims all over the world, who bow toward it while performing their prescribed prayers five times a day.

The hajj, or holy pilgrimage. Traditionally, the hajj takes place during the twelfth month of the Islamic lunar calendar. This calendar began on July 16, 622 (as expressed in terms of the Gregorian system), the day of the Prophet's flight from Mecca (Hijrah).

FACT FILE

Since AD 632, the Kaaba has been an exclusively Islamic shrine.
Circa 570
Birth of Muhammad in Mecca.
Grand Mosque
Area: 3,840,563 sq ft/ 356,800 sq m
Capacity (inside): over 800,000
Dimensions of the Kaaba: 39 × 33 × 49 ft/ 12 × 10 × 15 m

Left-hand page: The Kaaba in the Grand Mosque. During the course of the hajj, the pilgrimage to Mecca that is obligatory for all Muslims, pilgrims circumambulate the Kaaba seven times.

Right: In order to enable the countless pilgrims to symbolically stone Satan, several replicas of the stone pillar have been erected.

Below: Certain details of the "Great Pilgrimage" reveal a distinct ancient Arabic influence, in particular the concept of a "peace of God" around the shrine— a kind of right of asylum and guarantee of immunity.

Because the lunar year is shorter than the solar year, the dates of the months migrate. Dhu al-Hijjah, the month of the pilgrimage, is regarded as a holy month in the Islamic world. The climax of the pilgrimage occurs between the eighth and the thirteenth days of the month, when the "Festival of Sacrifice," Eid al-Adha, is celebrated. For this event, up to three million Muslims converge on Mecca, making the city the biggest place of assembly in the world.

Muhammad was a member of the Quraysh tribe, which traced its ancestry back to Abraham. In the early sixth century, this tribe took control of Mecca and the Kaaba shrine. The Prophet preached a message of one god (monotheism) and warned of the Day of Judgment, and in doing so, attracted ever increasing hostility. On July 16, 622, he fled with his supporters to Medina, only to return just eight years later as conqueror and make the Kaaba an Islamic shrine. The hajj, or annual pilgrimage, was eventually to become one of the most important rituals in the Muslim world.

Jamarat al-Aqaba. An impressive part of the annual hajj is the "stoning" of the stone pillar known as Jamarat al-Aqaba at another holy site in the vicinity of Mecca. The pillar symbolizes Satan and is "stoned" by the Muslim faithful.

Medina

AL-MASJID AN-NABAWI, OR THE "MOSQUE OF THE PROPHET," IN MEDINA IS THE
SECOND MOST HOLY SITE IN ISLAM. IT HOUSES THE PROPHET'S TOMB AND STANDS
ON THE SPOT WHERE MUHAMMAD HIMSELF BUILT A MOSQUE.

The first mosque was built next to the house in which Muhammad settled with his family when he arrived in Medina in AD 622. It was a rectangular unroofed building of roughly 98 × 115 ft/ 30 × 35 m with a raised platform from which the Qur'an was read. The walls were made of palm wood and mud. The mosque was entered through three doors: Bab Rahmah in the south, Bab Jibril in the west, and Bab al-Nisa' in the east. This basic ground plan has been re-created in every mosque in the world ever since. At that time, the direction of prayer (*qiblah*) was still north, toward Jerusalem. Only later was it changed to Mecca. In addition to being used for prayer, the mosque served as a court of law, community hall, and Islamic school.

Early enlargement. Just seven years later, this first mosque was doubled in size in order to accommodate a rapid increase in the number of believers. It was enlarged again in 707, when Caliph al-Walid demolished the old surrounding walls and built a new mosque that incorporated the Prophet's tomb. Over the centuries, the mosque was repeatedly expanded. This place of worship measured 276 × 328 ft/84 × 100 m. It had a teak roof and its walls were decorated with mosaics.

FACT FILE

Location of the mosque
Medina, in the province
of Madinah.
Capacity:
Over 500,000 worshippers.
AD 622
Construction of the
first mosque.
707
Mosque enlarged by Caliph
al-Walid. Over the centuries,
the mosque was repeatedly
expanded, resulting in a
total of ten minarets
with a height of up to
344 ft/105 m.

Left-hand page: The second
most important pan-Islamic
shrine after the shrine in
Mecca is that in Medina—
the place to which
Muhammad fled in AD 622.
The first mosque was built
next to his house.

Right: Mihrab in the mosque
of the Prophet. The mihrab
is a niche set into the wall of
a mosque that indicates
the direction of prayer
toward Mecca.

The Ottomans. The Ottomans, who governed
Medina from 1517 until World War I, also left their
mark. Sultan Suleyman I (1520–66) erected the northeast
minaret, known as the al-Suleymaniya, and under Sultan
Abdulmecid I (1839–61), the holy site was completely
rebuilt (except for the tomb of the Prophet) and enlarged.
A fifth minaret, the al-Majidiyya, was erected on the
western side.

Saudi Arabia. After the founding of the kingdom of
Saudi Arabia in 1932, the mosque was again extended.
Most importantly, additional accommodation for
the growing number of pilgrims was provided in the
immediate vicinity of the mosque. In the 1950s, two
further minarets and a library were added. The mosque
was most recently enlarged under King Fahd (1921–
2005) in order to keep up with the ever-increasing
number of pilgrims. It was also modernized through the
addition, among other things, of an air-conditioning
system. The present mosque is 100 times bigger than
Muhammad's original.

Below: Thousands of
Muslims breaking fast in
front of the mosque
during Ramadan.

The Australian Aborigines and indigenous peoples of Oceania live in harmony with nature and see themselves as an integral part of the world around them. For this reason, their most important shrines are natural phenomena such as mountains and caves. The religions of these peoples differ fundamentally from the Occidental faiths. Here, the indigenous populations believe not in a linear succession of events, but in nature's ever-repeating cycles.

AUSTRALIA &
OCEANIA

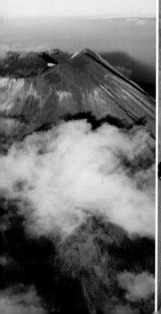

Uluru/Ayers Rock

ULURU, THE MONOLITHIC RED ROCK IN THE AUSTRALIAN DESERT, HAS BEEN THE MOST IMPORTANT SACRED SITE OF THE ABORIGINAL ANANGU PEOPLE FOR THOUSANDS OF YEARS. THE TRIBE ITSELF HAS LIVED HERE FOR OVER 10,000 YEARS.

T*jukurpa*, meaning "creation period" or "Dreamtime," is the word used by the Anangu to denote the origin of life. Under this creation myth, the ancestors entered the land as incarnations of man and beast (some slithered out of the depths of the earth as giant serpents), creating the landscape on their way. It was these ancestors who gave humankind the laws that are still observed by the Anangu today. The answers to every question concerning the origins of the universe and the laws of nature, the relationship between the sexes, life, death, and life after death are to be found in the myths and legends of the Dreamtime.

In the tongue of the Anangu, Uluru means "abode of the ancestors." Dotted along the monolith are sacred sites, of which some are reserved for male rites and others for female rites, while others are holy places for general ceremonies involving the participation of both genders. Each cave at the foot of Uluru has a specific meaning and has its own rituals associated with it. The caves are decorated with drawings relating to the rituals in question—some of these drawings are more than 3,000 years old.

The sacred sites of the Anangu. Under the spiritual laws of the local people, no one is allowed to

Uluru/Ayers Rock

At the foot of Uluru are sacred sites where the Aborigines perform their rites and rituals. These sites now enjoy higher levels of government protection than before.

set foot on the rock other than on ceremonial occasions. Nevertheless, hundreds of tourists climb the holy rock each day—half a million or so every year. The Aborigines observe the white visitors and refer to them as "ants" because of the way they climb Uluru in a line, clinging to the steel cable that guides them to the top. Climbing the rock is actually extremely hazardous. A combination of high temperatures and sudden changes in the weather causes a number of fatalities and injuries each year.

The first white man to climb the monolith was the engineer William Gosse in 1873, during his exploration of the northern territories of Australia. He named it after the premier of South Australia at the time, Sir Henry Ayers. His discovery of the outcrop perpetuated a tendency that had been present ever since the first Europeans set foot on the continent: a disdain for the culture of the indigenous peoples. Over recent years, however, things have started to change. Uluru was handed back to the Anangu on October 26, 1985, and it is now forbidden for tourists to enter the national park during the

Anangu rituals—indeed, the park remains closed for the duration. In order to promote respect for the sacred sites of the local people, the photographing of certain specially marked sacred sites, most of which are located at the foot of Uluru, is now prohibited. Infringements are punishable by heavy fines.

FACT FILE

Height:
1,142 ft/348 m
Circumference:
5.8 miles/9.4 km
Width:
1.5 miles/2.4 km
Length:
2.2 miles/3.6 km
Age
Formed around 600 million years ago. Uluru, composed of arkose (a type of sandstone), is the second-largest monolith on earth (Mount Augustus in Western Australia is the largest).
1987
Inscribed as a UNESCO World Heritage Site.

Far left and left: A local man, and visitors climbing Uluru. It is not uncommon for visitors to be unaware of the culture of the indigenous Australian peoples.

Rurutu, Austral Islands

CAPTAIN JAMES COOK DISCOVERED THE ISLAND OF RURUTU—THEN CALLED
ETEROA—IN 1769. THE ISLANDERS LIVED IN CAVES, GROTTOS, AND UNDERGROUND
PASSAGES, AND PERFORMED THEIR SACRED RITUALS IN MYSTERIOUS CEREMONIAL
PRECINCTS KNOWN AS *MARAE*.

The present inhabitants of Rurutu no longer live in caves, but nevertheless remain committed to their traditions. The island, with its countless caves, grottos, and mineral-rich high plateaus, is surrounded by cliffs that rise up vertiginously from the ocean. Since time immemorial, the islanders have practiced the mystical art of stone lifting, a feat of strength whereby fragments of rock weighing up to 330 lb/150 kg are raised in the vicinity of the island's *marae*, or sacred sites. The Pareopi and Vitaria marae, which until recently were still used by the royal family of Rurutu, are dominated by the island's characteristic pillars of stone that soar into the heavens. During the Tere ceremony in January, a large procession makes its way across the island to the sacred marae and other mystical sites, including the grottos of mythical man-eater Hina and giant lizard Mo'o. The festival ends with a stone-lifting competition in which both male and female athletes compete.

Sacred sites of an unusual kind. Marae, the most famous of which are probably Easter Island's *ahus*, are found on every island in the archipelago of Oceania. As well as being the location for other ceremonies, the sacred stones were the venue for prayers for protection from the

Rurutu •

Left-hand page: The lush tropical flora of the Austral Islands.

Below: In 1769, almost exactly ten years before his death, the English explorer Captain James Cook (1728–79) witnessed a human sacrifice on a Polynesian marae.

elements and for sacrifices to the gods. However, they are unusual in not having been used solely for religious rituals: Courts were held, and political and social decisions taken here. Many of the marae were taboo and could only be entered by priests, for only they were capable of establishing communication with the heavenly powers. Human sacrifice was not uncommon at the large marae. Many marae were ringed by undecorated stone columns and *tikis*, or statues of the gods. The tikis are always male, powerful, mysterious, and protective, with folded arms and legs, head tilted backward, and no neck. Furthermore, a lot of sculptural attention is paid to the genitals in order to emphasize them. The role of tikis is to afford protection and fend off danger.

Above left and right: Tikis are always male, powerful, and mysterious, with folded arms and legs, head tilted backward, and no neck.

FACT FILE

Location
Rurutu is situated 355 miles/ 572 km southwest of Tahiti and has an area of 12 square miles/32 sq km.

When Captain Cook discovered Rurutu in 1769, the island had around 3,000 inhabitants. Christianization from 1821 onward, diseases imported from the outside world, war, and emigration have reduced the population to a little over 2,000.

There are three villages on the island: Moerai, Avera, and Hauti.

NEW ZEALAND

The Sacred Mountain of Tongariro

FOR THE MAORI, WHO ARRIVED IN NEW ZEALAND IN ENORMOUS CANOES
AROUND 750 YEARS AGO, THE VOLCANO TONGARIRO WAS A SACRED MOUNTAIN
ON WHOSE SUMMIT A FIRE HAD TO BE LIT IN ORDER FOR THE NEWCOMERS TO TAKE
POSSESSION OF THE LAND.

Some 750 years ago, the Maori journeyed in large outrigger canoes from eastern Polynesia to present-day New Zealand in several waves of emigration. One of the legends of this "indigenous" people of New Zealand tells of Chieftain Ngatoroirangi going ashore in the middle of North Island to claim the land. In order to do this, he had to climb the volcano Tongariro and light a large fire at the top. He was accompanied by his faithful slave girl, Auruhoe. On the snow-capped summit, it was so cold that the pair almost froze to death. The chieftain invoked the

help of the priestesses of the mythical place Hawaiki, beseeching them to send him fire. The priestesses, who were his sisters, obliged with a fire that broke out off the coast, ran under the water, and ended up licking the chieftain's feet at the top of the mountain. In order to thank the god of the volcano, Ngatoroirangi threw his slave into the crater as a sacrifice. One of the three volcanoes in the national park was subsequently named after her: Ngauruhoe. According to Maori mythology, Hawaiki is the home of volcanoes, but it remains unclear whether it was a real island or a purely mythical place.

A wise decision. The end of the eighteenth century saw the first *pakeha*, or white people, arrive in Aotearoa,

The Sacred
Mountain of
Tongariro

FACT FILE

Tongariro National Park
Established in 1894.
Three volcanoes: Tongariro,
Ngauruhoe, and Ruapehu.
Mount Tongariro was given
to the government on
September 23, 1887.
Height range of volcanoes:
1,640 ft/500 m–9,177 ft/
2,797 m
Area: 307 square miles/
795 sq km
1990
Inscribed as a UNESCO
World Heritage Site.

Above left: The water in the
crater of Ruapehu Volcano,
one of the three peaks of
the Tongariro Massif, is
iridescent and transparent.

Above: Ngauruhoe is
named after the slave girl
of Chieftain Ngatoroirangi,
whom he sacrificed to
the god here.

the land of the "long white clouds." As a result of intensive
sheep farming, clear-cutting, and brutal treatment of the
native peoples, the land of the Maori around their sacred
mountain was in danger of becoming barren. The sacred
Mount Tongariro is where the Maori's ancestors lie buried,
and the claim of the Maori to mountain and country was
legitimized by their proximity and the constant presence
of the deities of their nature religion. Many of their most
sacred places are to be found on the mountain even today.
There was no stopping the white settlers, however. They
encroached more and more, taking what belonged to the
local people and desecrating their holy places. In order to
avoid losing their land completely, Chieftain Tukino Te
Heuheu made a wise decision. In 1887, he presented the
sacred mountain to the government as a gift. The only
condition was that it had to be preserved for all people.
Tongariro thus became the world's fourth national park.

Right: Ferns, the oldest
plants in the world, thrive in
the undergrowth throughout
Tongariro National Park.